CATS
TO THE
RESCUE

CATS
TO THE
RESCUE

True Tales of
Heroic Felines

by *Marilyn Singer*

with illustrations by Jean Cassels

Henry Holt and Company ☟ New York

To my talkative cat, August

Many thanks to my husband and best critic, Steve Aronson, to my wonderful editor Christy Ottaviano and the Holt crew, and to the following folks who were so generous with information: Dr. Sally Rhine Feather (Rhine Research Center), Carol Markt, Brad Steiger, Judy Robbins, and Betty Royse.

Henry Holt and Company, LLC
Publishers since 1866
175 Fifth Avenue
New York, New York 10010
www.henryholtchildrensbooks.com

Henry Holt® is a registered trademark of Henry Holt and Company, LLC.
Text copyright © 2006 by Marilyn Singer
Illustrations copyright © 2006 by Jean Cassels
All rights reserved.
Distributed in Canada by H. B. Fenn and Company Ltd.

Library of Congress Cataloging-in-Publication Data
Singer, Marilyn.
Cats to the rescue : true tales of heroic felines / by Marilyn Singer; with illustrations by Jean Cassels.—1st ed.
p. cm.
Includes bibliographical references (p.).
ISBN-13: 978-0-8050-7433-8 / ISBN-10: 0-8050-7433-3
1. Cats—Anecdotes. 2. Cats—Behavior—Anecdotes. 3. Rescue work—Anecdotes. I. Cassels, Jean, ill. II. Title.
SF445.5.S56 2006 636.8'0887—dc22 2005034856

First edition—2006 / Designed by Laurent Linn
Printed in the United States of America on acid-free paper. ∞
1 3 5 7 9 10 8 6 4 2

Contents

Introduction

There are twelve animals in the Chinese zodiac. The cat is not one of them. Here's a legend about how this came to be. Cat and Rat were friends. So when the Buddha announced a contest to assign each animal an hour and a year, the two made a pact: Whoever got up earliest would rouse the other, and together they'd win the competition.

But the next day when Rat awoke he did not keep his word. He left Cat sleeping and hitched a ride with Ox. Just as they arrived at the Buddha's gate, Rat jumped off and dashed in to gain first place.

Cat slept on through the whole morning. When she finally did awaken, she let out a yowl and raced to meet the Buddha. But it was too late. The whole zodiac had been filled. That's why there is no Year of the Cat and why cats and rats are now sworn enemies.

It is certainly true that cats are great sleepers. For that reason they've unjustly earned a reputation for being lazy. They are also great hunters. Hunters need to rest a lot in order to be able to run and leap and seize prey at a moment's notice. A leopard would not be able to carry prey nearly as heavy as itself up a tree if it did not have a great deal of stored energy. So a dozing house cat isn't a couch potato—it's just conserving its energy in case a rat comes along.

Hunting is probably what brought cats and humans together, just as it did dogs and people. But dogs have had a much longer relationship with us. Twelve to fifteen thousand years ago, wolves somehow joined people at campsites to feed and to hunt with their human companions. This social relationship makes sense because canines and people both prefer to live in groups. A wolf's group is called a *pack*. Each pack has a leader and a pecking order—from top dog down to the lowest member of the group. The lower-ranked members are willing to obey their superiors. In a household, those superiors tend to be the humans. From these ancient wolves, domestic dogs evolved. Over the centuries, people have created many varieties of dogs to perform a wide range of jobs. Today it's hard to look at a poodle, a golden retriever, or a Chihuahua and see the wolf it once was.

Cats still look much like their ancestor, the wildcat (*Felis sylvestris*), though they are now much smaller—and they act quite a bit like the wildcat, too. At least five thousand and perhaps as much as ten thousand years ago, these wildcats were drawn to villages, probably in what is now

WILDCAT   DOMESTIC CAT

the Middle East, where homes and food-storage buildings attracted rodents. The felines moved in, and humans let them stay. Soon they were brought by boat to islands and countries all over the world. It became common to have cats on ships to protect food supplies from rodents. Some felines may even have been on the *Mayflower* in 1620 when the ship landed in the colony of Massachusetts. We do know that fourteen years later in *New England's Prospect* William Wood wrote about how cats saved the colony's crops from squirrels and what we now call chipmunks.

Throughout their history, felines have been loved, feared, and hated. In ancient Egypt, cats were worshipped. In the Middle Ages in Europe, many were tortured and killed. As their popularity began to rise again, humans created a number of breeds—they mated cats that had desirable characteristics in order to pass along their genes until they established Persian, Siamese, Rex, and other cat varieties. But these breeds don't vary as much as dog breeds do. After all, felines are not raised for the jobs canines perform. Also, their genes will not allow for great changes in size and other physical traits.

Nowadays, some cats live lives of luxury, while others scrounge for food on the street. There are still people who misunderstand them, claiming that all felines are sneaky, aloof, even nasty. Other folks know that cats share common traits and skills such as the ability to climb, stalk, and scratch, but that they do have individual personalities.

Like their wild ancestors, cats continue to be largely loners. They can live together in groups, but they have no leader or even a pecking order. They obey no one but themselves. However, they are intelligent and adaptable, so they know a good thing when they see it. Through watching, listening, and learning, they've come to appreciate and even love their human and sometimes their animal companions.

We certainly love them in return. Today the cats in households outnumber dogs, probably because quite a few of these households have multiple cats. Felines give us affection and entertainment—and sometimes more. A lot more. A surprising number of cats have turned out to be role models, therapists, and lifesavers. Their heroics usually spring from their feline traits and abilities. But sometimes their bravery and compassion seem to come from sources we can't understand.

Among them there was Towser, whose hunting skills made the *Guinness Book of World Records*; Simon, winner of the Dickin Medal for bravery during wartime; Sugar, who spent fourteen months trekking from California back home to Oklahoma, 1,500 miles away; Grover, who saved his family from a fire; and Precious, survivor of the World Trade Center attacks. Their stories inspire us to view and celebrate cats in new ways.

So, in honor of the "thirteenth animal of the Chinese zodiac," let me introduce you to a group of fascinating felines. Some are ordinary, others extraordinary, several are legendary, most are real—but each and every one is a hero.

Chapter 1

Mighty Hunter

DICK WHITTINGTON'S CAT

Once upon a time, there was a poor boy named Dick Whittington. He went to London to seek his fortune. Instead, he ended up in the house of Sir Hugh Fitzwarren, a rich traveling merchant, where he slaved in the kitchen for the mean cook and lived in a tiny room overrun by rats. Dick had hardly any money, so he was thrilled when one day he earned a whole penny for cleaning a man's shoes. What did he buy with the precious coin? Sausages? Strawberries? New boots? No. Dick bought a cat.

And what a cat it turned out to be! Every night the boy shared his meal with Puss. In return, it rid his room of rats. Soon it set to work on the rest of the house. Sir Hugh was impressed. He called Dick to him and said, "I would like to buy that cat." Dick felt a tug at his heart. He did not want to part with his only friend. But Sir Hugh was his master, and when the man offered six times what Dick had paid for the feline, the boy could not refuse. He bid a sad good-bye to his companion, and the cat set sail with the merchant on his ship.

In Arabia, Sir Hugh, as was his custom, went to the sultan's palace, but he did not receive the usual royal welcome. "I am most embarrassed," the sultan explained. "Rats have eaten all the food. I can offer you nothing."

"But I have something I can offer *you*," said the merchant. He fetched the cat and loosed it in the palace. Puss immediately went to work.

The sultan was amazed. "I must have that mighty hunter!" he exclaimed. So he bought the cat for a fortune worth ten times the ship's cargo.

Now Sir Hugh, believe it or not, was an honest man. Upon his return to England, he gave all the money to his astonished kitchen boy.

His fortune made at last, Dick Whittington married the boss's daughter and then went on to become the mayor of London, all thanks to his cat! As for Puss, no one can say for sure what had become of her, but chances are she drank cream and slept on silk cushions in the sultan's palace for the rest of her life.

Or so the legend goes . . .

There really was a Richard Whittington who served as mayor of London three times between 1397 and 1420. Did a cat really help him find his fortune? Nobody knows.

Just as nobody knows if a cat named Acater actually saved Sir Henry Wyatt's life. When he was a young man, Sir Henry made an enemy of King Richard III, and in 1483, the monarch imprisoned the lord in the Tower of London. Dressed in rags, with only a thin straw mat for a bed, Sir Henry lay cold and hungry in the miserable dungeon. He would surely have taken ill or starved to death if it hadn't been for Acater. One day the cat paid him a visit and curled up on the man's chest to keep them both warm. *Perhaps I will not die after all,* Sir Henry thought.

From then on, Acater came every day, and not just to sleep. As often as she could, the cat would bring him a pigeon she had caught. Sir Henry asked his jailor if the man would be willing to cook the birds. The kindly jailor took pity and agreed.

Two years later, when Richard III was killed, the new king pardoned Sir Henry and released him from prison. He went on to become a wealthy, happy man, the Keeper of the Royal Jewels and the Treasurer of the King's Chamber, and he lived a very long time. A portrait of Sir Henry and Acater hangs in the home of one of his descendants. The Wyatt family castle still stands, and cats are always welcome. As for Acater, we assume she met a happy end.

PREDATOR!

Dick Whittington's and Sir Henry Wyatt's cats may be legends, but we know that millions of real live cats *are* mighty hunters. Cats are built to hunt. Among their superior senses, they have excellent eyesight. They have a wider field of vision than humans do, so they can accurately judge where their prey is. Their large, light-sensitive eyes, like their wild cousins, are for night hunting. A cat's pupils contract to slits rather than circles. This allows them to control more precisely the amount of light that enters their eyes and also to protect their retinas. The pupils also have a reflective layer called the *tapetum lucidum* that helps cats see better in darkness—and makes their eyes shine yellow-green in car headlights or flash photographs.

No cats can see in total darkness, though, any more than humans can. Although recent research shows that cats are not color-blind, scientists believe that color doesn't mean much to felines. After all, it doesn't help them find a mouse or enjoy a bowl of tuna.

Hunters need to be stealthy and flexible. Cats can move swiftly and silently on their padded paws. Their spines are elastic and they can turn their forelegs in almost any direction. Cats have approximately thirty-eight more bones than we do (depending on the length of their tail), but they lack a collarbone. That means they have narrow chests and are able to squeeze through tight spaces. Along with the ability to jump and pounce, all cats have a superb sense of balance. Their tails help stabilize them when they pace a ledge or make a quick turn, but tailless cats are good fence walkers, too.

To capture their prey, hunters need effective weapons. Cats have ten front claws that can be whipped out to snare a bird or rodent and thirty pointed teeth to kill it, then cut and tear the meat. They shed their worn-out nails by regularly scratching them on trees, posts, and sometimes furniture. This helps keep their claws razor sharp.

Felines hunt and kill animals for food, but they also capture animals they can't eat, such as toads and shrews, which are poisonous. Hunting small animals trains a cat to snare the next tasty house mouse or rat that appears. When a cat catches a rodent or other animal, it will often "play" with it, patting, swatting, tossing, or letting it escape, only to catch it again. Some scientists think this behavior makes sure the prey won't attack, and it also prepares the cat for the kill—a bite on the back of the prey's neck.

PRACTICE MAKES PERFECT
Cats hunt by instinct, but they need practice to become experts. When kittens play with each

other, they are practicing hunting behavior. But their main teachers are their mothers. Mother cats bring prey, first dead, then alive, to their kittens so they can work on their pouncing, seizing, and biting. Sometimes cats think we are their kittens, and they will bring prey to us. Perhaps that is what Acater was doing for Sir Henry.

Cats' hunting skills have kept them alive for thousands of years, way before there was canned cat food. They caught mice, rats, and other prey in the wild and then in granaries, barns, warehouses, and homes. People came to respect felines' ability to protect their food supplies, as well as their plants, mail, art, books, and even silkworm cocoons, from vermin. These mighty hunters have helped save families, businesses, and entire countries from disaster—and people paid well for their services.

WORTH THEIR WEIGHT IN GOLD

In tenth-century Wales, King Hywel understood the value of cats so well that he passed a law fixing their worth. A champion "ratter" had the same value as a fourteen-day-old foal, a six-month-old calf, or a young pig. Anyone who stole or killed a cat had to pay for it. The penalty was either a sheep, a lamb, or the amount of corn that completely covered the feline's body if the cat was held by the tip of its tail so that its nose touched the ground. In the 1870s, the miners of Deadwood, South Dakota, were having such a mouse problem that they were eager to buy cats from traveling salesmen for gold dust. Some cats sold for twenty dollars, a huge sum in those days, or at least that's what the salesmen claimed to their customers.

About half a century ago, the World Health Organization (WHO) sprayed the insecticide DDT in the island Borneo to kill mosquitoes that carried malaria. The insects died, but they were eaten by geckoes, which in turn were eaten by cats. Poisoned by the insecticide, the cats also died, and rats began to flourish. So the WHO created Operation Cat Drop and parachuted fourteen thousand felines into Borneo. The costly operation saved the people's rice crop and protected them from two rat-borne diseases, typhus and plague.

CATS AT WORK

Although many respected hunters have been nameless, others have achieved fame in books and on the Internet. For nearly twenty years at the beginning of the twentieth century, a popular cat named Mike protected books from mice in the British Museum library. Cats no longer live there, but many other libraries, as well as bookstores and even hotels, have working cats.

In the 1930s, Rusty was the first cat to have a job at New York City's Algonquin Hotel. He cleared rooms of mice and greeted guests. The latest Algonquin cat, Matilda, was a great mouser when she first came to the hotel. She would catch rodents and deposit them on the front desk — sometimes as guests were checking in! Now exterminators do most of the mousing, and Matilda spends her time welcoming people, riding the elevators, and occasionally sleeping in the guests' rooms. She gets lots of fan mail and has a birthday party each year.

Cats have traditionally served as "mousers" and companions on ships and in lighthouses. They protected not only the food supplies but the wooden structures themselves from being gnawed by rodent teeth. Many of these felines were well known in their time. The most famous American lighthouse cat of all was nineteen-pound Sambo Tonkus. During the 1930s, he entertained visitors at the Cape Neddick "Nubble" Lighthouse in Maine by swimming from the Nubble to the mainland. There, after playing with feline friends, he'd catch a mouse and swim back to the lighthouse with the rodent in his jaws.

Then there was Towser, perhaps the greatest hunter of them all. The Glenturret Distillery in Scotland uses barley to make whiskey. Towser worked there for nearly twenty-four years, keeping this grain safe from mice. In her lifetime she caught 28,899 mice, which she apparently left for the staff to find, and she made the *Guinness Book*

of World Records as the World Mouse-Catching Champion. To make this record official, only the mice found near the stills were carefully counted. No one calculated the number of rats and rabbits she also caught. When she died in 1987, a statue was erected in her honor.

Nin and Percy don't have statues—at least not yet. But these popular mousers work in locations somewhat stranger than a hotel or a distillery. Mount Washington, New Hampshire, boasts "some of the world's worst weather." And there's an observatory there to prove it. Besides heavy snow, bitter cold, and frequent fog, the mountain is often hit by fierce winds. In fact, the highest wind velocity ever officially recorded anywhere in the world occurred there on April 12, 1934— 231 miles per hour! Scientists live and work at the facilities, but the only full-time, year-round resident is the Observatory (Obs) cat, currently Nin.

This black-and-white feline is an important member of the crew. He keeps down the mouse population and makes the research center more homey. Although he is unlikely to venture outdoors during a winter blizzard, he does run around the

peak as soon as the storm clears because the high winds blow away most of the snow. Nin also takes advantage of the summer sun, especially since the temperature never gets above a pleasant 72 degrees. In 2003, a generator fire knocked out power to the observatory and forced crew members, including Nin, to evacuate. But the cat has since returned to duty as the mountain's one and only "snow leopard."

Percy also scales the heights—in a plane. The Bengal cat performs his mousing duties in the Ameristar Air Center at the Roseburg Regional

Airport in Oregon. Percy is a carnivore, but unfortunately he has a taste for sweets as well. He loves doughnuts and has been known to break into the freezer in the lobby to steal ice cream bars. But his dedication to hunting and his personality have made the cat such a favorite with pilots visiting the lounge that some have taken Percy up in their planes. And what does the cat think about his trips in the air? Percy's boss Shannon Rives says, "He likes to sleep in the flight bag. He's very relaxed about the whole thing."

To people around the world, Mike, Rusty, Nin, Percy, the record-breaking Towser—and millions of other mousers—are heroes worth their weight in gold.

Chapter 2

War Hero

SIMON

The cat was hungry. He didn't complain when Lieutenant Commander Bernard Skinner, captain of HMS *Amethyst*, rescued him from the Hong Kong Harbor, took him back to the British escort ship, and named him Simon.

On board there was plenty of food to eat and the captain's comfortable bunk to sleep on. Lieutenant Commander Skinner was so fond of the cat that he even allowed Simon to pad across the table when he was charting a course. For a year, Simon lived a life of ease. Besides being the captain's companion, his main job was to entertain officers and their guests with his party trick: fishing ice cubes out of the water pitcher.

Then, on April 19, 1949, the captain was ordered to head up the Yangtze River. China was in the midst of a civil war between the Nationalists and the Communists, and the *Amethyst's* job was to guard the British embassy at Nanking and, if necessary, to evacuate it. Though it was a dangerous time, the crew didn't expect their ship to be attacked. But early the next morning, the Communist forces opened fire. Shells pounded the wheelhouse and the bridge. Men lay dead or wounded, Lieutenant Commander Skinner among them, and the ship ran aground. Simon had been asleep in the captain's cabin when it took a direct hit. The cat was thrown into the air by the blast and knocked unconscious. One of the sailors picked him up and carried him to safety, but no one expected him to last the night.

Another officer managed to get the ship afloat, and the *Amethyst* hobbled two miles upstream. The attack stopped, but the ship was badly damaged and the next day Lieutenant Commander Skinner died. With the *Amethyst* unable to move and the ventilation system ruined, the heat was unbearable. As if that wasn't bad enough, the food supplies were being raided by rats. By the time the new captain, Lieutenant Commander Kerans, arrived, things looked bleak.

Then something amazing happened. Simon had not only made it through that first night, but just a few days later he was well enough to begin a new job: hunting. When he caught his first rat, the crew cheered. For the next three months, with the *Amethyst* still grounded, he caught a rat each day. But that wasn't Simon's only task. He also visited the crew, particularly the wounded, to give them comfort. As their spirits lifted, the men worked during those months to repair the ship.

Then Lieutenant Commander Kerans decided the *Amethyst* was ready to make a daring escape. During the night of July 30, covered in black canvas, with the anchor chain muffled in grease and blankets, the ship slipped away. Although the Communists fired on it from the shore, the *Amethyst* raced ahead and reached open water. On November 1, it sailed into the harbor at Plymouth, England, to a grand heroes' welcome.

The crew insisted that Simon was the true champion of the Yangtze Incident. All of Great Britain agreed. Simon was given the Dickin Medal for bravery in wartime, the only cat ever to win that award.

ON THE LAND, ON THE SEA, IN THE SKY

Simon was certainly a war hero, but he was not the first cat to serve during wartime. A legend says that 2,500 years ago, Cambyses, a Persian king, knew that his Egyptian enemies worshipped cats. So he told his soldiers to hold up live cats as shields. The Egyptian army refused to attack them and was defeated. Other cats were used throughout history in battles to detect poison gas or to spread it (bottles were attached to their backs, and they were chased toward the enemy). But the best-known wartime cats were mascots like Simon, whose duties were hunting and raising morale.

Another mascot named Oscar seemed to prove the myth that cats have nine lives. Oscar was originally a crew member on a famous German battleship, the *Bismarck*, during World War II. When the ship was sunk in 1941, Oscar was found swimming nearby. A British sailor rescued him and brought him aboard HMS *Cossack*. Five months later, the *Cossack* sank. Once again, Oscar swam for his life and became the mascot of the *Ark Royal*, an aircraft carrier. When that ship was hit by torpedoes, Oscar survived once more. But his seafaring days were over. He retired to a sailors' home, where he never had to swim again.

Other cats took to the skies instead of the seas. During World War II, Windy was the pet of Wing Commander Guy Gibson. He brought luck and comfort when he flew in the dangerous and successful Dambusters raid during which British pilots blew up German dams to cut off electricity to the Nazis.

In *Amazing but True Cat Tales*, Bruce Nash and Allan Zullo tell of another Second World War flying cat. Captain Ed Stelzig adopted a black-and-white stray and named him Adolf because the black patch under his nose looked like Adolf Hitler's mustache. On board Captain Stelzig's plane, Adolf had his own litter box and a resting place atop the warm radio equipment. When the plane landed, he'd jump out and return only when he heard the engines start up. Once he boarded the wrong plane and ended up five hundred miles away from the captain. But they were reunited. By the end of the war, Adolf had flown more than 92,000 miles. Captain Stelzig gave him to a colonel's children who dearly loved him. Adolf was probably just as happy to snooze on their beds as to fly in a C–47.

Why have cats made such good mascots during warfare? Besides their valuable hunting skills, many cats are calm under pressure. That helps soldiers, sailors, and other military men and women stay calm, too. During quiet times, the felines' often amusing behavior prevents the crew from becoming bored. Cats are also small and portable—they fit into tight spaces such as ship and airplane cabins.

Cats have a strong sense of place. They are good at finding their way home and staying there, whether that place is a cabin, a castle, or

army barracks. In 1942, during World War II, Mourka lived in the Russian army headquarters in Stalingrad. A long and dreadful battle was going on in that city. The commander knew that Mourka would run from the fighting to the headquarters, so he gave the cat to a gun crew stationed near the front. When it became too dangerous for scouts to take messages to headquarters, the crew chief would fasten a message to Mourka's collar and then let him go. Upon reaching safety, the cat was always greeted with treats and petting.

For several months, Mourka was called upon to do his duty, but then he disappeared in action.

Though it was a sad end for a war hero, Mourka undoubtedly saved lives on his missions. The *London Times* wrote, "He has shown himself worthy of Stalingrad, and whether for cat or man there can be no higher praise."

Chapter 3

World Traveler

SUGAR

Sugar did not want to ride in the car. Perhaps she remembered that last big trip, just over a year ago, when she'd had to leave her beloved home in Oklahoma and travel all the way to California. Now her owners were moving back to the Sooner State, and Sugar was about to face another 1,500-mile journey.

The Woods family was packed and ready to go. "Come on, Sugar. It won't be so bad," one of them probably said. *Yes, it will,* Sugar yowled. The cat protested so much that the family reluctantly decided the best thing would be to leave her in California with their neighbors, who were very fond of the cream-colored Persian. With great sadness, the Woodses headed back to Oklahoma. Fifteen days later, so did Sugar.

The distressed neighbors wrote that Sugar had disappeared. The Woodses were devastated. Everyone was sure the cat had died. Then, one day, fourteen months later, in 1952, Mrs. Woods was busy in the barn when a cream-colored Persian jumped through the open window, landed on her shoulder, and rubbed against her neck. The startled woman called for her husband. *It can't be, can it?* she wondered. As a kitten, Sugar had been in an accident that caused her hip to be crooked. Mr. Woods hurried over and ran his hand along the cat's side. Sure enough, he felt the familiar deformed bone, easily identifiable by a veterinarian. Sugar—a cat who had never wandered farther on foot than her neighbor's bushes—had crossed the desert and the Rocky Mountains and faced countless dangers to come home at last.

HOMING HOWIE, TREKKING TOM

Besides Sugar, there have been many incredible feline travelers. Howie was another Persian who made a trek almost as long as hers. In 1977, fifteen-year-old Kirsten Hicks and her family were excitedly planning a long trip from Adelaide, Australia, to Europe. It was too bad that they couldn't bring Howie along. Kirsten wanted to make sure her cat was in good hands. The only people she trusted to watch him were her grandparents, one thousand miles away on the same continent. "Sure, we'll take care of him," they agreed. So, Howie went off on his long vacation, and Kirsten and her family went on theirs.

It wasn't until the Hickses returned from Europe to collect their cat that Kirsten's grandparents gave them the bad news—Howie was gone. Kirsten didn't blame them for Howie's loss, but every time she thought of her beautiful cat, she wanted to cry. How could a spoiled baby like Howie ever survive on the street?

Perhaps she was still thinking about him a year later, when a scruffy Persian showed up on her doorstep. Though the reports do not say how she was certain, Kirsten knew it was Howie. Taking him into her arms, she burst into tears. As for the cat, he didn't cry. He was too busy purring.

How on earth did Sugar manage to cross the United States or Howie make his way over the vast Australian outback? How do any cats make such incredible journeys? This question has intrigued people for years. Over short distances, cats certainly use their senses of sight, hearing, and smell to find familiar territory. But what about long distances? Some scientists wonder if cats' homing instinct is related to the ability of birds and other creatures to migrate. They think that migratory animals have a sort of compass in their brains that allows them to follow the earth's magnetic fields when they travel to and from their winter and summer homes. Perhaps cats, too, use these fields.

That might explain how felines can find their way back home. But what explains how some cats can find their owners in places these felines have never been? Tom is a remarkable example. His owners, the Smiths, believed that cats are more attached to their homes than to their people. So they felt that Tom would live a happier life in familiar surroundings. In 1949, when they decided to move from Saint Petersburg, Florida, to San Gabriel, California, the couple gave the cat to the man who bought their old house. Two weeks after they arrived at their new home, they learned that Tom had run away.

One day, a little over two years later, Betty Smith heard a cat yowling in their yard. Her husband, Charles, went out to chase it away. But the cat leaped into his arms. "Tom!" he gasped and carried him indoors. The cat was skinny and ragged. Its fur, bleached by the sun, was falling out, and its paws were sore and bleeding. It was so weak it collapsed on the kitchen floor. Betty wasn't certain this poor creature was Tom, but she remembered that the cat had been raised on baby cereal and had an unusual taste for a brand called Pablum. She rushed out to the store to buy some, then returned, prepared the cereal, and set a dish near the exhausted animal.

Staggering to his feet, he stuck his face in the food and began to gobble it down. Though it may be that a hungry cat would eat anything, Betty was convinced this fellow was indeed her Tom. He had somehow survived a 2,500-mile journey, the longest recorded for a wandering cat, across the whole United States to find the people he loved.

PSI-TRAILING

Dr. Joseph Rhine of Duke University came up with a term for treks such as Tom's: "psi-trailing." Dr. Rhine and his associate, Dr. Sara Feather, were able to document over twenty cases of true psi-trailing cats. In all of them, the owners were able to identify their pets by markings, old injuries, habits, or other means. One feline they documented was Clementine, who traveled 1,500 miles from Dunkirk, New York, to Denver, Colorado, in 1949 to find her owners, the Lundmarks. They had left her behind on their farm because she was pregnant. After Clementine's kittens were weaned, she took off and appeared three months later at their front door in Denver. They recognized her by the seven toes on her front feet, a scar on her left shoulder, and two unique white spots on her belly. In addition, their veterinarian confirmed that she had had kittens.

In their study, Drs. Rhine and Feather also described Beau Chat, a white half-Persian, who took over a year to travel from Lafayette, Louisiana, to Texarkana, on the Texas-Arkansas border, nearly three hundred miles away. The cat's favorite child was named Butchie, and when Beau Chat arrived in

Texarkana, he went straight to the boy's school. Butchie knew him at once by the scar over his eye, the nick in his ear, and the smear of tar on his tail. As if those marks weren't enough, there were other definite signs that this was indeed Beau Chat. The feline had been raised by the family's collie, along with her pups, and had learned to growl and bite like a dog when angry. He also came when someone whistled. Sure enough, the wandering cat showed all of these responses. Not only did his human family recognize him, but so did the collie!

So far, no one has been able to explain what enables cats to make this type of journey. Is there a telepathic connection between owners and their pets so that humans somehow communicate to animals where they are and how to get there? Are the cats themselves psychic? Do they have a special sense, triggered by loneliness or desperation? Whatever the answer, if being a hero means facing obstacles and refusing to give up, then these cats live up to the name.

Chapter 4

Adventurer

ZIGGY

They say a long journey starts with a single step. Ziggy's five-thousand-mile trek certainly began that way—but it also involved traveling by canoe, bicycle, and backpack.

His adventure began in October 1990, when he met Jim Adams. Just a few days before, Jim, a former paramedic, had set out on a triathlon vacation. Part one would be a two-thousand-mile canoe trip down the Ohio and Mississippi rivers. He was camping along the Ohio banks when Ziggy, just two months old, bounced over from a neighboring farm. The man and the spunky gray tabby got along so well that Jim asked the farmer if he could adopt Ziggy. From then on, they were inseparable.

Ziggy was fearless. He wasn't bothered by

dogs, coyotes, raccoons, or people. He loved canoeing. He even liked water. Each evening, he would leave the campsite and wade into the river to try to fish. He enjoyed hiking just as much—and that was fortunate because part two of the vacation was a hike along the Appalachian Trail, more than 2,100 miles of it, through fourteen states from Georgia to Maine.

In sun, rain, and snow, Jim and Ziggy climbed mountains, walked across meadows, and splashed through marshes. Sometimes Ziggy chased insects; other times he went mousing. One night, at the Blood Mountain Shelter, he caught eleven mice. He ran along with Jim until he got tired or the weather turned nasty. Then the cat would jump onto the backpack and let Jim carry him, too. At the start of the long trip, Jim weighed 212 pounds. By the end, he'd lost fifty-seven pounds. Ziggy, on the other hand, went from three pounds to fourteen—a hefty addition to Jim's already bulky backpack. When the pair reached Maine, Ziggy officially became the first cat ever to cover the entire Appalachian Trail.

But their journey wasn't over. They still had the last part of their triathlon to finish—nine hundred miles by bicycle. Just as he'd taken to canoeing and hiking, Ziggy relished bike riding. He savored standing on a saddlebag and feeling the wind in his face. By bicycle he and Jim traveled from Bar Harbor, Maine, to Webster, Pennsylvania, where Jim's journey had begun a year before. Like his companion, Ziggy had become a great athlete—or maybe we should call him a cathlete!

CLIMB EVERY MOUNTAIN

There have been and still are mountaineering cats. From 1910 to 1919, a feline named Ginger liked to trail along with visitors climbing Mount Taranaki in New Zealand. On January 16, 1917, Ginger's owner, Harry Williams, a trail guide, was leading a party of five women up the mountain. Ginger tagged along. He made it all the way to the top on his own four paws. Harry took photos and gave the cat a certificate to prove it.

Eleven years later, a stray calico named Hilda joined a group of hikers on Mount Blumlisalphorn in the Swiss Alps. She was adopted by the mountaineering club and moved into their shelter, located at nine thousand feet. One day Hilda decided to follow some climbers to the summit. Although she had to be carried part of the way, she did reach the peak — 12,038 feet above sea level. From then on, Hilda made a lot of climbs. Sometimes she'd stay atop the mountain and greet the next arrivals. Sadly, Hilda was there alone when she disappeared during a snow storm. But she remained a legend for many years.

More recently Tomba, a cat named after the well-known Olympic skier Alberto Tomba, also scaled several of the Alps. Born in 1988, Tomba lived with guide Otto Stoller and his family at the Schwarenbach Inn and was only ten months old when he made his first climb. Though he died of an illness at the age of four, Tomba is still famous among mountaineers.

It's not really surprising that so many cats enjoy mountain climbing and other adventures. Cats are curious creatures. They have to be. They

need to explore and learn everything they can about their surroundings to find the best hunting and sleeping spots, to learn who and what are their enemies, to discover what food is available, and many other things. Male cats will establish and mark their territory and patrol it regularly to warn off other males and to lure females. Females will find secure hiding places to give birth. At the same time that they need to explore, cats also want familiarity. Both males and females will use well-known sights, sounds, and smells to retrace their steps, and they prefer to follow the same trails over and over. Therefore, the Alpine cats mentioned above made great guides.

Although cats do not follow a pack leader the way dogs do, they still become attached to their owners, and they often enjoy the company of others as well. Some people feel that cats see their owners as kittens. Others believe that cats view themselves as kittens and that they want to re-create the same comfort and safety they felt when they were young. Whatever the reason, they are willing to hike trails and ride in or on bicycles, canoes, motorcycles, and even surfboards if it means they can be with the folks they like.

Chapter 5

Smoke Detector

GROVER

It must have been Grover's cat-show training. For several years he'd dealt with all that bathing and brushing, all those judges who examined him to see if he was worthy of a prize. Now that the lovely Siamese had retired, he was willing to put up with little Lynn Tanner's

idea of grooming— dressing him up in doll clothes and then pushing him in a carriage. He even allowed her to pick him up by the tail and hold him like a baby, as long as every night he got to sleep on her pillow.

One night in the late 1970s, Grover proved he was more than just a beautiful cat. Four-year-old Lynn and her parents, Johanna and Roger, were fast asleep when their intercom shorted out and started a fire. Poisonous smoke filled the house. The family dog had passed out, and the Tanners were nearly unconscious, too.

Grover knew he had to do something. Although he could have escaped to the balcony, he decided to stay and awaken his people. Jumping off Lynn's pillow, he dashed into her parents' room and ran up and down on their bed. Then he hurried to the bathroom and knocked tubes and bottles off the counter. Still the Tanners didn't get up. So he raced back to Lynn's room. *Wake up, wake up,* he urged, walking all over her and scratching and biting her arms and hands. Lynn awoke at last and started to cry.

The sound of her daughter's distress roused Johanna. With enormous effort, she woke up her husband and managed to get Lynn, Grover, and the dog out of the house. By the time the fire department arrived, Roger had put out the flames. The firefighters cleared out the fumes with fans and let the family know when it was safe to re-enter the house.

The Tanners put Lynn back in her room, but Grover wouldn't let her stay there. So he and the girl, who was wrapped in a sleeping bag, joined her exhausted parents in their bedroom. Through the rest of the night, Grover kept checking the intercom to make sure the fire was really out. He was one terrific smoke detector, and he never needed batteries.

WAKE-UP CALL

When we think about animal heroes, we usually picture dogs—guarding, protecting, and saving people from dangerous situations. And it's true that among animals, canines most often come to the rescue. But Grover and many other cats have shown themselves to be lifesavers, too. Take a silver tabby called Winter.

In 1999, Victoria Kennedy was sharing her fifteen-year-old daughter Faye's bedroom while hers was being redone. The pair were asleep when a candle they'd forgotten to put out set the dining-room curtains on fire. Rex, the family dog, was, apparently, too terrified to move. So it was up to Winter to save them all. Like Grover, he tried yowling to wake them, but Victoria and Faye thought he was just begging for breakfast and ignored him. Next, the cat clawed at the blankets and stepped on Victoria's face. She pushed him away and kept sleeping.

Winter knew it was time to try something Victoria hated. He didn't scratch or bite. He licked her face. Cats's tongues are covered with small barbs to help scrape every bit of meat from the bones and skin of their prey and also to help remove dirt from themselves when they groom. Winter's scratchy tongue must have felt like sandpaper on Victoria's tender skin. Sure enough, she awoke, smelled the smoke, and roused Faye. Mother, daughter, and their pets fled just before the house burst into flames.

SUPER SNIFFERS

A good smoke detector like Winter or Grover is helped by a great sense of smell, and cats are superb sniffers. They are not as talented as dogs are, but they are much better at detecting odors than humans are. Their noses are about twelve times more sensitive than ours. We have between five and twenty million scent receptor cells. Cats have over sixty million. They also have a special structure called a *Jacobson's organ* that enables them simultaneously to taste and smell the air when they open their mouths. When a cat uses this structure, it rolls back its upper lip and wrinkles its nose. This odd-looking practice is called *flehmen*. The expression may look funny to us, but it's serious business to a cat. Cats flehmen most often when they are looking for mates, but they probably do so under other circumstances as well. With their noses and their Jacobson's organs, cats can detect smoke long before we can. They can even notice scents we can't smell at all.

DRUMMING FOR DANGER

That feline detective ability helped solve a mystery that could have turned deadly. Carol and Ray Steiner adopted an orange kitten. When he wanted attention, the cat would drum his paws on the glass kitchen doors. So the Steiners named him Ringo after Ringo Starr, the famous drummer of the Beatles.

In 1995, two years after Ringo moved in, the Steiners were having a rough time. Ray was recovering from heart surgery, and Carol had hurt her leg badly in an accident. They began to develop strange symptoms, including high blood pressure and great fatigue. They blamed their health problems on the surgery and accident. But instead of getting better, they got worse. Soon they could barely think clearly or stay awake.

One afternoon when they were napping, Ringo began to slam his body over and over against the front door. In a daze, Carol finally got up to let him out. "Ringo, what on earth is wrong with you?" she demanded. In response, the cat ran around the house and then returned, asking her to follow. "You're just going to lead me to a dead mouse," she said, but she decided to hobble after him. He led her to an area near the gas meter. He dug and dug through a layer of sharp rocks. A distinct odor began to rise from the ground. Now Carol could smell it, too—and identify it. It was an underground gas leak. "We're going to explode!" She screamed for her husband, but he couldn't wake up. Carol called the gas company, and the technician found a broken fitting, right where Ringo had uncovered it. The fumes had been seeping into the house for months. No wonder the Steiners had gotten sick.

After the leak was repaired, Carol and Ray got well. They were not the only people Ringo had helped. The Steiners' gas pipe was connected to pipes in six other houses. They all could have exploded. The cat's detective work had saved the lives of twenty-two people. Ringo was awarded the William O. Stillman Award for Bravery from the American Humane Society—and the deep gratitude of the Steiners and their neighbors.

EARLY WARNING SYSTEM

Besides a great sense of smell, cats also have excellent hearing. They can hear much higher-pitched sounds than we can—up to fifty thousand cycles (we can hear up to twenty thousand, the highest notes on a violin, for example)—and from all directions, which is how they can locate mice and other prey. We can barely move our ears, but cats can turn theirs a full 180 degrees. During World War II many cats alerted their owners about air raids long before the sirens sounded. During these raids, people would put on masks to protect themselves from poison gas, dust, and debris. Sally, a cat who lived near the London docks, would leap at a gas mask hanging in the hall. Then she'd run back and forth from the mask to her owner. Once they got outside, Sally would scratch at the air raid shelter door. After her owner was safely inside, she'd hurry next door to warn the neighbors. Then, at last, she'd enter the shelter, too.

A cat named Bomber could even tell the difference between British and German airplane engines. When he recognized a German plane, he led everyone to the air raid shelter. He probably learned to distinguish the sounds initially by watching people's reactions to them.

But a cat doesn't use only its ears to hear. Many scientists think that cats also "hear" with the soles of their feet. They can feel the vibrations when a mouse runs across the floor — or when an earthquake or a volcanic eruption is about to occur. Some scientists believe that cats don't use sound to sense a catastrophic event, but instead detect changes in the earth's electrical fields. However they do it, for years felines have been used in some countries to predict natural disasters. Hours before a quake or an eruption, they may become restless and look for places to hide. Mother cats will move their kittens to safety.

There's a report of a cat named Toto who, in 1944, warned his owners that Mount Vesuvius in

Italy was going to erupt. All afternoon he'd been agitated and unwilling to eat. That night the normally sweet and friendly cat awoke Gianni, his master, by scratching his cheek. He kept attacking the man until he got out of bed. Gianni's wife, Irma, was deeply religious and saw Toto's behavior as a sign from heaven that the volcano was about to erupt. She insisted that they leave. Gianni protested, but at last he agreed. The couple packed and fled their house in the nick of time. Mount Vesuvius did erupt—and the lava and ash destroyed not only their home but their whole village. Here's hoping Toto was with them!

In 1975, when the cats and other animals in Haicheng, China, grew nervous, officials wisely evacuated the city. The next day there was a huge earthquake. Buildings were severely damaged, but many lives were saved.

Grover, Winter, Ringo, Bomber, Toto, and the cats of Haicheng all used their senses to act as smoke detectors, air raid wardens, and seismologists. Some cats have won medals for their life-saving abilities. Others have used their talents to become heroes in a different field—medicine.

Chapter 6

Emergency
Medical Technician

WHEEZER

Nothing was wrong with the kitten in the window. Though he seemed to be wheezing, he was simply tasting the air. But Gary Fielding instantly identified with him. Gary really did wheeze. He had asthma and often needed an inhaler—a small pump—to spray medicine into his mouth so that he could breathe. The inhaler worked much faster than the pills he also took. Gary was not allergic to cats, so he decided to get the kitten and give it his own nickname, Wheezer.

Wheezer was the perfect pet. Curious and friendly, he was especially alert to Gary's asthma attacks. Sometimes he'd just stare at the man. Other times, after a bad attack, he'd pat his friend's cheek or stand on Gary's lap to taste his breath.

One afternoon Gary had a severe attack. He needed his inhaler immediately. But he couldn't find it. The harder he searched his apartment, the more terrified he became. Where could the pump be? He took his pills, lay down on his bed, and tried to calm down, but his chest was tight and it was hard to breathe. Then he heard a strange clattering. Looking up, he saw Wheezer heading toward him, batting something across the floor. *Oh, Wheezer. This isn't playtime,* he may have thought. But it wasn't a mouse or a toy that the cat was whacking. It was the precious inhaler! Gary got up, grabbed the pump, and sprayed medicine into his mouth.

At once he felt better. Sitting on the floor next to his pet, he asked how the cat knew what he was looking for. In answer, Wheezer climbed into his lap and put his paw on Gary's lips. Perhaps he was saying, "Trust me, I know *everything* about you."

LIFESAVERS

Smoke and gas fumes are not the only things that smell strange to a cat. Inhaler spray probably does, too, at least initially, until the cat gets used to the odor and realizes the spray is something its owner uses regularly during an asthma attack. Gary Fielding's doctors told him that when Wheezer tasted his breath, the cat was probably using his Jacobson's organ to identify the scent of the inhaler. Centuries ago, people did not know about this organ. They believed that cats weren't tasting air, but sucking the breath out of people, especially children. They also thought that felines would smother babies by lying on their faces or chests. Neither is true.

Gary Fielding's story, reported in *Hero Cats* by Eric Swanson, shows how a cat can use its sense of smell and taste to help someone. These keen senses, along with sight and hearing, may also explain how some cats are able to detect seizures, choking, and other dangerous conditions. To cats, humans smell, taste, sound, and look different when we're sick or hurt.

A Siamese named Shoo Shoo must have used

one or more of his senses to help several disabled residents at Able, Inc., in North Dakota. His owner, Karen Brazelton, who worked at the home, brought the cat to live there because he was lonely—Karen and her husband worked all day, and their grown children had moved out of the house. Shoo Shoo enjoyed his new residence. The cat's amusing antics, such as stealing pens and sipping drinks from people's glasses, brought him the attention he craved.

But one morning Shoo Shoo seemed to go mad. He raced around, meowing, and threw himself over and over at Karen, who is hearing impaired. He insisted that she follow him to one of the rooms. When she opened the door, she found that a patient was having a seizure. From

then on, Shoo Shoo regularly patrolled the house and fetched Karen whenever he found a person in danger. He was a reliable guardian. He alerted her to a woman with a serious liver problem and to another resident having seizures. Often, he would keep watch to make sure the person was feeling better again before he took a well-deserved nap.

When Bob Gilliland adopted a tabby named Joy from a shelter, he never expected the cat would repay him with more than a happy purr. The retired fire chief was diabetic. One night his blood sugar was too low. Unable to yell, he was slipping into a coma. Sensing that something was wrong, Joy ran from the living room, where she usually slept, to the bedroom and began to yowl until Bob's wife, Lura, awoke to help him. Did Joy smell chemical changes in Bob's body? Did she hear his weak cries for help? Or did she use all her senses to recognize that her owner was in very serious trouble? In any case, we've all heard many stories about firefighters rescuing cats, but this may be the first time a cat rescued a fireman!

Another reason felines can spot danger is that they spend a lot of time studying humans to understand our behavior. For example, Wheezer must've seen Gary Fielding using his inhaler and figured out what it was for. Cats' powers of observation can startle us, especially when we don't realize how closely we've been watched. This kind of surveillance may explain the case of another amazing lifesaver: Gandalf.

RING FOR ASSISTANCE

Like Joy, Gandalf was a shelter cat. He'd been abused by his previous owner, which probably accounted for his shyness. But he loved his present owner, Margaret Howieson. Margaret and Gandalf lived in a senior citizens home in Scotland. One day in August 2001, Margaret had a stroke. She needed help. If only she could make it to the living room, she could pull the alarm cord. But both her legs were paralyzed. For an hour she tried and failed to get out of bed. *What am I going to do?* she thought, letting out a frustrated groan.

The sound awoke Gandalf, who'd been sleeping on her bed. He sized up the situation at once.

He had to have noticed that alarm cord before. Maybe he'd seen Margaret use it on occasion. Running into the living room, the cat leaped into the air and tugged the cord with all his might. Then he waited for warden Isobel Craik to arrive. When she did, he impatiently led her to the bedroom and followed her around as she took care of Margaret and called for an ambulance. Margaret was taken to a hospital. When she and Gandalf were reunited at the home, she told him over and over what a good and clever cat he was. Gandalf stared back at the woman with his big eyes. "I know," he seemed to say. "I know."

Gandalf was not the only bell-ringing feline. According to *Cats Incredible!* by Brad Steiger, Trixy, a small Abyssinian, loved to ring the dinner bell outside W. A. Bigelow's home in Kansas. But the constant clanging annoyed the neighbors, so W.A. tied the rope out of Trixy's reach.

Then on December 8, 1977, the elderly man fell on the walkway in front of his house and broke his hip. He lay there for some time until Trixy found him. He told her he needed help, then laughed at himself for talking to a cat. It turned out to be the smart thing to do. Trixy hadn't rung the dinner bell in a while, but she knew it was the best way to bring out the neighbors. Jumping three feet into the air, she grabbed the rope and swung back and forth until, sure enough, folks came out of their homes to complain about the noise—and to rescue her owner. While W.A. recovered in the hospital, Trixy was cared for by his son and daughter-in-law and praised for being the hero she was.

Salem, featured in *Hero Cats*, also liked the sound of a big bell. This one was hanging above a milk can on Martha Agrelius's porch in Pennsylvania. It was magic, that bell. It made Martha and her neighbors appear, and Salem enjoyed their company and attention. Then, to the cat's dismay, Martha decided to raise it out of his reach.

One icy February day, Salem was wandering outside and he discovered his owner lying in her driveway. Her face was cold, and her head was bleeding. She couldn't get up, but she was able to open her eyes and look at the cat. Salem understood at once what he had to do. Climbing on top of the milk can, he gathered his strength. Then he sprang high and higher still into the air until, clunk, he hit the bell. Martha claimed she heard him ring it nearly a dozen times before an irritated neighbor finally appeared.

While Martha recovered from her injuries—a broken hip and a head wound—Salem received many treats and toys. For years to come, Salem's, Trixy's, and Gandalf's owners would be able to talk about what it was like to be truly saved by the bell.

Chapter 7

🐈

Mother

SCARLETT

The flames were fierce. The black smoke was choking. There was no time. The cat had to hurry and save herself. But she couldn't leave. Not without her kittens. Time after time, she returned to the burning building. One by one, she carried out her five babies. Then, despite her burnt fur and paws, she began to move them from outside the ruined and vacant auto shop to a safer place across the street.

By the time David Gianelli of Ladder Company 175 in Brooklyn, New York, found her, she'd already managed to rescue three kittens and was returning for the others. Once they were all out of harm's way, the kind fireman gathered the family into a box. He said that even though her eyes were so blistered that she could not see, the mother cat touched every kitten with her nose to make sure she had not lost a single one.

The fireman took the cats to the North Shore Animal League on Long Island. Under the shelter's care, the mother, now named Scarlett, and all except one of the kittens survived. Eventually they were placed in good homes. Their story made the news around the world. People everywhere were touched by the saga of the brave stray cat who'd saved her family.

MAMA WILL PROVIDE

Of all feline mothers, Scarlett is probably now the most famous. Her story, which took place in 1996, was featured in newspapers, on television, on the radio, and even in an entire book. But nearly sixty years earlier, another mother cat was also a celebrity. Her name was Faith, and she won two special civilian medals from British and American humane groups for her courage during World War II's terrifying Battle of Britain. Faith lived with Reverend Ross, the rector of a church in London, England. She was famous for greeting churchgoers before services. She also liked to march down the aisle and curl up by the rector's feet during his sermon.

In the summer of 1940, Faith gave birth to a single kitten named Panda. Although she had a comfortable bed in the rector's room, she insisted on carrying Panda down into the basement. One night when the rector was out of town, the church was bombed. He heard the news and hurried back to London to look for Faith and Panda. The rectory lay in ruins. The firemen told him that the cats couldn't have survived. But Reverend Ross was determined to search. When he neared what was once the basement, he heard a cat answer his call. Digging through the rubble, he found Faith wrapped around her baby. Both mother and kitten were alive and well. Faith's story spread throughout Britain as a message of hope and comfort during a difficult time.

Some wonderful cat mothers were not so well known as either Scarlett or Faith. In 1970, a cat named Princess saved her kittens from drowning. A cruel person had put the mother and babies in a burlap bag and thrown them into a creek. Princess tore open the sack and carried three kittens to safety. An eleven-year-old paperboy passing by helped rescue a fourth. In 1985, during a fierce thunderstorm, I watched my own cat, Miss Kitty—a stray who'd arrived pregnant just a month before—bring her kittens through the window from the garden into the house. She dropped each on the rug in front of me. I stood guard to make sure our dogs didn't trample them.

All four of these cats were good mothers. Why? The answer is a combination of instinct and upbringing. Cats, like all animals, need to reproduce, to make more of their species. It is in cats' nature to feed and defend their kittens, to teach them to hunt and to survive on their own, and, when they are ready, to send them out into the world. This instinct is so powerful that many cats will place their kittens' safety above their own. Because they have such a strong urge to mother, some cats will raise orphaned animals of other species—even if those animals are ones that cats would normally hunt. Sophie, a white stray in Cardiff, Wales, fed two orphaned squirrels along with her single kitten until the squirrels could be weaned. The cat seemed to be bothered by nothing about them except their huge, fluffy tails. Felines have also been known to raise rabbits, rats, and mice as if they were kittens.

To make sure the kittens thrive, mother cats must not only nurse them but keep the litter together. A mother cat will grab a kitten by the scruff of the neck and carry it back to an old nest or off to a new one. If she moves all the kittens, the cat will return once more to make sure that none have been left behind.

But not all mothering comes from instinct. Scientists hypothesize that when kittens have good mothers, they grow up to be better mothers themselves. So, we can guess that even if they didn't save their families from fire, bombs, water, or thunderstorms, the mothers of Scarlett, Faith, Princess, and Miss Kitty were strong, brave, and caring—hero mothers in their own right.

Chapter 8

Bodyguard

SYBIL

Sybil the Siamese cat was nine-year-old Pam Price's baby. Her very *big* baby. The three-year-old feline weighed twenty pounds! Like little Lynn Tanner's cat, Grover, Sybil didn't seem to mind playing the role. She always let Pam push her around in a carriage.

And that's where Sybil was as Pam went strolling one day in 2001 from her home in the suburbs of Detroit, Michigan, to her friend's house a few blocks away. Neither of them noticed the stranger in the dark four-door automobile driving slowly beside them.

Suddenly the man slammed on his brakes, flung open the door, ran out, and grabbed Pam. He slapped tape across her mouth and tried to drag her into the car. Struggling, she managed to reach into the carriage and pull out Sybil. The normally peaceful cat instantly went wild. She clawed the man's arm ferociously. The kidnapper let go of Pam and reached into his pocket. Did he have a knife? A gun? Whatever it was, he never got it out. Sybil leaped onto his chest and bit his throat. He flung the cat to the sidewalk just as Pam's neighbors appeared with bats, walking sticks, and golf clubs and surrounded the felon. Someone had phoned the police; another had called Pam's mother, who quickly arrived to comfort her daughter. The assailant was arrested and later jailed.

As for Sybil, the big baby climbed back into the carriage for a well-deserved snooze.

ATTACK CATS

A guard dog is not a rare creature. Domestic dogs are naturally protective of their pack, which usually consists of their human family and companion pets. Without being told what to do, they may bark, growl, and even bite to defend the pack. Canines can also be trained to protect under orders. Police and other guard dogs are taught to attack only on command, and when they do so, they generally go for the perpetrator's arm and not his throat.

Cats aren't interested in protecting a pack. In the wild, most types of cats are loners. But they will defend themselves, their kittens, and sometimes their people and other companions. When Sybil attacked the kidnapper, she was probably startled and protecting herself. She may also have been defending *her* baby—Pam. That was most likely the case with two other outstanding bodyguards, Shade McCorkle and Booboo Kitty.

The year was 1932, and Nell Mitchell was having a bad day. The eighty-eight-year-old Memphis resident was ill. Dr. Longset had given her an injection, but he was worried about leaving her alone for the evening. "It's all right," Nell apparently told him. "My husband will be home soon." *Besides*, she may have thought, *I have Shade*

McCorkle for company. The doctor would not have believed the gray tabby to be of much help, but he had other patients to see and so he left.

Nell and Shade were drifting in and out of sleep on a lounge in her kitchen when an intruder entered the house. First he asked for food. When Nell said she was too sick to fix him a meal, he demanded her wedding ring. Nell did not want to part with something so precious, but she was frightened. Pulling off the ring, she offered it to the thief. He seized it and struck her across the face.

When he raised his hand to hit her a second time, Shade burst out from under the blanket. Jumping onto the thief's shoulders, the cat sank his teeth into the man's neck. The intruder ran around the room, punching Shade and scream-ing, "Call him off!" The tough cat hung on—even as the man tried to strangle him. When Shade managed to scratch his face, the thug threw the tabby to the ground. But Shade attacked again. Finally, the man grabbed the cat and dashed him against a table. Then he ran out of the house.

He didn't get far. The police captured him. Nell and Shade recovered from the ordeal, and the cat won the Latham Foundation Gold Medal for heroism.

Booboo Kitty's adventure, reported in the *New York Times* and other news media, began on an ordinary December evening in 2003. Leonard Rzep-nicki and his wife, Cheryl Walker, were entertaining some friends in their Manhattan apartment. They were gathered in the kitchen, cooking dinner, when there was a knock at the door. It was a neighbor and an unknown man. Leonard let them in. Little did he realize that the stranger had forced the neighbor at gunpoint to lead him there.

The gunman demanded money. But none of the six friends had any. Angered, the thief made them all take off their clothes, and he ordered Leonard into the bedroom. That was Booboo Kitty's cue to appear. Leonard asked the gunman not to hurt the cat, but the brute grabbed her. With a hiss, Booboo Kitty scratched his hand. The gunman dropped the cat and chased her into the living room.

Though he was naked, Leonard seized the opportunity to escape. He ran out of the apartment and down two flights of stairs, where a neighbor let him in to call the police. The gunman was still in Leonard's apartment when the cops arrived and shot him. Wounded but alive, the assailant was taken to the hospital. Though they were frightened and embarrassed, Leonard, his wife, and friends were unhurt. "I really think that cat saved my life," he told the reporters. What he might not have realized is that Booboo Kitty, like Sybil and Shade McCorkle, had also saved her own.

THE AMAZING AGGIE

Perhaps the most amazing bodyguard of all is a calico cat named Aggie. She lives with well-known runner and writer Lynn Seely and her husband, John. One snowy night a prowler approached their Pennsylvania home. Aggie was the only one awake. She knew instantly that something was wrong. Later on, Lynn claimed that the cat obviously hadn't cared for the sneaky way the screen was removed. "She didn't like the cold air pouring in; she especially did not like the smell of this strange, menacing person who was standing just outside *her* window!"

The burglar stacked up two cinder blocks and climbed into the house. As his head came through the window, Aggie attacked. His face scratched and bleeding, the man screamed and fell backward, accidentally leaving a shoe on the windowsill before stumbling away.

Lynn and John were awakened by the shriek. Cautiously, they headed downstairs. In the living room, they discovered the open window and the telltale shoe, and they immediately phoned the police. As they waited for the cops to arrive, Aggie strutted over. "She was fluffed up larger than I'd ever seen," Lynn said. "She turned towards me with her tail swishing back and forth as it did when she was really happy about something."

It took Lynn a bit of investigating to figure out why Aggie was so pleased with herself. The policeman confirmed Lynn's deduction. As he patted the cat, he told Lynn and John that the thief had robbed other houses in the neighborhood, but he'd always chosen homes that didn't have dogs. "Guess he never reckoned on an attack cat," the policeman probably said.

One more thing about the one and only Aggie—she was not only courageous, but she was also totally blind!

BURGLARS, BEWARE!

This chapter wouldn't be complete without the story of a British tortoiseshell named Bonnie. She wasn't a human bodyguard, but she was one of the most outstanding security guards to make the news. In 2001, a pair of burglars broke into a warehouse. What were they planning to steal? Several tons of dog food! They had loaded only a few bags into their truck when the six-year-old cat caught them and attacked. Though the robbers tried to fight off the feline, she scratched and bit until they were forced to flee.

At least that's what the police think happened. Warehouse owner Mike Powell called them after finding the place in disarray, with missing bags of food, streaks of human blood, and a slightly injured but proud cat. "Bonnie's a real beauty and worth her weight in gold," said Mike. "You don't need a guard dog with a tiger like her about."

Many dogs and their owners can thank that particular tiger for protecting their chow. As the next chapter shows, some other dogs can be grateful to several cats for saving their lives.

Chapter 9

Pet Protector

SPARKY

If cats and dogs are supposed to be enemies, that
was news to Sparky and Lacy Jane. The calico
cat and the toy poodle got along perfectly well.

It was a sunny October day in 1990 in Dora,
Alabama, when Teresa Harper let out Lacy Jane
into their yard. Sparky was taking a typical snooze
on a ledge and dreaming cat dreams. Teresa had

barely gone inside when she heard the frightening sounds of growls and yelps. Racing to the door, she was horrified to see a pit bull with its teeth around her poodle's throat. Teresa gasped, sure that the smaller dog was a goner.

But Sparky knew better. Awakened by the commotion, the cat let out a hiss, then jumped ten feet from the ledge smack onto the pit bull's big head. Now it was his turn to yelp. Digging her claws into the dog's skull, Sparky held on as tight as, in Teresa's words, "a rodeo rider on a bucking bronco." She refused to let go until the pit bull at last flung her off and ran away.

Teresa ran over to Lacy Jane. The poodle was bleeding badly, but her owner got her to the vet in time, and she survived, all thanks to her little protector, Sparky.

Dogs can learn to view cats as part of their pack, and cats will accept dogs and sometimes even see them as good company. I've long kept canines and felines as pets in the same house. My current standard poodle, Oggi, often has friendly, noisy wrestling matches with my long-haired tortoiseshell cat, August. Cats and dogs in the same household learn to read each other's body and vocal language. They may have spats—for example, Oggi is very lively, and when he jumps too vigorously on August, she will swat him, but they generally get along. However, some cats seem to go beyond mere toleration or harmony, and it's hard to explain why.

A FRIEND IN NEED . . .

According to Brad and Sherry Hansen Steiger in *Cat Miracles*, Taco, a rat terrier, was ten when J. M. Escobedo and his family got a gray cat named Big Boy. Taco and Big Boy didn't hit it off right away. In fact, they hated each other and frequently fought. But as they got older, they became close friends, especially when the dog lost his sight.

One afternoon in 1996, when J.M. was on the porch reading the paper and Big Boy was having a snack next to his chair, Taco began to wander out of the yard. The man wasn't paying attention, but the cat was. He saw that his buddy was heading for a cliff that overlooked a beach. If Taco fell, he'd be seriously injured or even killed.

With a yowl, Big Boy dashed off the porch and reached the dog just in the nick of time. Blocking Taco's path, the cat answered his whine with a friendly meow. Taco seemed to understand that Big Boy was offering to help him. The gray tom moved from one side to another, nudging the dog along, leading him home. J.M. watched the whole rescue in wonder. He knew of visually impaired people who had guide dogs, but this was the first time he'd ever seen a blind dog with a guide cat!

Another touching story in *Hero Cats* concerns Frankie the dog and Johnny the cat. Frankie was a middle-aged Labrador mix who lived with Geoff Watson's family. He took an immediate liking to the tabby kitten the Watsons adopted from a Massachusetts shelter. The two played many games, ate meals side by side, and even slept together. But their playtime was eventually hampered when Frankie's eyesight and hind legs began to fail. Soon the dog could hardly stand up. Geoff was sad to see his pet's health decline. The pooch was eating less, too, but to Geoff's surprise, he didn't seem to be losing weight. The man began to suspect that somehow Frankie was stealing the cat's food. So he moved the bowl from the floor to the kitchen counter.

For several days after, he'd find the bowl back on the floor with the food scattered about. How was his crippled dog managing to knock it off the counter? Geoff decided to spy on his pet. But instead he fell asleep and never heard the bowl fall. What woke him instead was, as he put it, "a strange sort of skittering sound." Peering into the kitchen, he saw the overturned bowl. However, it wasn't Frankie who'd knocked it down. It was Johnny. To Geoff's astonishment, the cat was batting his kibble over to Frankie, and the dog was eating whatever came his way. It was heart-warming enough to make Geoff want to cry—but funny enough to make him laugh instead.

That Johnny fed Frankie is surprising, since he was a male cat and not a mother. But there have been incidences of toms caring for kittens and other animals. Sheila Burnford's Simon, who was the role model for Tao, the Siamese cat, in her well-known book *The Incredible Journey*, helped raise an Abyssinian kitten with pneumonia, a litter born to an ineffective mother cat named Anna-belle, and an Irish setter puppy.

LIFEGUARD

Cats have rescued or befriended other animals besides puppies and kittens. Recently Puss Puss, a black-and-white tailless cat, accompanied her owners, Adrian Bunton and Karen Lewis, a pair of gardeners, to their job at a home in Icomb, England. As Adrian and Karen worked in the garden, the cat became upset and ran back and forth, meowing, between them and the swimming pool. Adrian and Karen followed Puss Puss. There, floundering in the water, was a lamb that had escaped from its flock in a nearby field. After the couple rescued the lamb from drowning, Karen told reporters that her lifeguard cat was "a real little superstar."

. . . IS A FRIEND INDEED

A cat named Cat was intrigued by a creature even larger than a sheep. At the age of six weeks, in 1995, the tiny orange tabby walked into a grizzly bear's enclosure at Wildlife Images, an animal rehabilitation center in Oregon. The kitten, along with his mother and two siblings, had been dropped off at the center a few days before. Griz, the bear, had been there a lot longer—since 1990. His mother and sister had been killed by a train as they foraged for spilled grain on the tracks. Griz had also been struck. He was blinded in one eye and had some nerve damage. Though he survived, his injuries meant he could never be released in the wild. On top of that, he had become dependent on humans. He cried if he was left alone. J. David (Dave) Siddon, founder of Wildlife Images, was his only friend.

Dave was watching helplessly by the gate to the compound the day that Cat entered. He was certain the bear would swallow the kitten along with the lunch he was devouring. Cat seemed unaware of his impending doom. Purring, he approached the bear. Griz turned and looked at him. The kitten froze. The two stared at each other until the bear returned to his meal. Cat edged closer and closer. Dave held his breath. Then Griz reached into his lunch bucket, pulled off a small piece of chicken, and dropped it in front of the feline. The kitten grabbed the food and ran under a bush. And that was the beginning of a beautiful friendship.

Cat and Griz slept together, chased each other, and played a variety of other games. The cat rode

on the bear's back, and Griz even carried him around by the scruff of the neck, like a mother cat with her kitten. The bear no longer needed Dave's constant companionship. He'd found a new buddy. As for Cat, he had the best protector any feline could imagine. Who on earth would pester a puss with a 650-pound grizzly bear guardian?

Such animal friendships are a delight and a puzzle. How do they occur? No one is sure, but scientists do think that timing and circumstances are important. When animals meet and how they've been raised account in part for how they get along. A kitten is more likely than an adult cat to bond with a bear. On the other hand, some adult cats such as Big Boy become more fond of canines—or other creatures—with age. It's as if they're saying, "Well, I put up with you for so long, I guess I actually like you now." That not only makes the cats and dogs happier, but pleases their human companions, too.

Chapter 10

Therapist

DIXIE

Everyone gets tired sometimes, even bouncy teen-age girls. But Caroline Berry of Brundall, England, was beyond tired. She felt as though she didn't have an ounce of energy in her body. Her dear friend, Tilly, a tortoiseshell cat, had been hit by a car. Doctors diagnosed Caroline's problem as chronic fatigue syndrome, an illness, possibly triggered by grief over Tilly's death, that made her exhausted. She had to be hospitalized, and she missed months of school.

Enter Dixie. The pretty calico cat, adopted from a shelter, won over Caroline's parents, Gail and David. She soon won over Caroline, too. The girl began to teach Dixie tricks—how to beg, give a paw, and fetch straws. It became clear that the feline was doing more than entertaining

her new owner—she
was healing her. Since
the cat joined the fam-
ily in 2003, Caroline
has had fewer and
less severe attacks.
"Dixie is what gets
me up in the morn-
ing when I am low,"
she told a reporter for
Evening News 24. "Before I got

her . . . I would just stay in bed all the time, and
now when I go downstairs, I get mobbed by her."

Dixie, whose name comes from *dix*, the
French word for ten, because she is the Berrys'
tenth cat, was a finalist for the prestigious Best
Friend Award given by the Cats Protection
League. Although she lost to another feline, Dixie
is still a winner, especially in Caroline Berry's
eyes.

A CAT A DAY KEEPS THE DOCTOR AWAY

In homes, schools, hospitals, rehabilitation cen-
ters, and other places around the world, there are

thousands and thousands of cat therapists. A number of studies have shown that pets promote good health. Stroking them helps relax people and even lowers their cholesterol and blood pressure. Some patients, such as Caroline Berry, have had more dramatic recoveries. How do cats help people recover from physical, mental, and emotional disabilities? By being themselves.

It's true that not all cats make good therapists. The best ones are generally calm, affectionate, and predictable. They like to be handled, and they won't bite or scratch. They enjoy the warmth from our bodies, and they love being petted. Petting probably makes them feel like kittens being groomed by their mother's rough tongue. Some cats, such as Dixie, are happy to learn tricks. Others prefer to lie in people's laps and purr. Groups such as the Delta Society in the U.S. and the Cats Protection League in Great Britain evaluate cats to see if they'll make good therapy animals. In New Jersey, Saint Hubert's animal shelter sponsors an animal-assisted therapy program. One of its most successful volunteers is Sandra Campbell, a nurse who has long visited senior citizen and nursing homes, veterans hospitals, and other health facilities with her cats, the best known of which have been Spunky and Ralph. Sandra adopted both felines from Saint Hubert's. She trained Spunky, a gray tabby, to lie on a towel. She'd bring the towel along on their visits. Wherever it was placed—on the floor, a bed, a table, a patient's lap—there Spunky would stay. His calm behavior helped soothe elderly patients and allowed them to open up and talk about themselves. Ralph, an orange tabby, soon joined the team, and the pair began to alternate visits.

One extraordinary day, Spunky was sitting in the lap of an elderly woman with Alzheimer's, a disease that makes a patient lose memory and often stop speaking. The woman smiled at the puss and proclaimed, "Pretty cat." The next week, when Ralph arrived, she said, "My, what a handsome cat this is!" The nurses were thrilled. It was the first full sentence the woman had spoken in years.

To honor Spunky and Ralph's work, the Delta Society awarded them its Lifetime Achievement Award in Animal-Assisted Therapy in 1995.

DRAMATIC RECOVERIES

Carol Markt's cat Joey has been a popular feline therapist in Oregon. When he rides in a cart down hospital halls, patients, staff, and visitors gather around to pet him. Carol can tell many tales of how Joey has helped patients. She says he's been working for about six years and has done some amazing things, including comforting a girl who's had medical issues for the past five years following a bone marrow transplant and cheering a woman with cancer who was so depressed that she had decided she didn't want to pursue a course of lifesaving treatment. To everyone's surprise, when Carol put Joey in her lap, the woman was so moved by the cat that she decided to get the treatment after all.

One of Carol's favorite stories involves another cat, Rocky. Eight years ago, he visited a teenage girl who'd undergone brain surgery. The girl was not responding to anyone or anything. After Carol put the girl's hand on him, she began to scratch his chin. Rocky had accomplished what no one else had been able to.

In *Your Incredible Cat*, David Greene tells of a

ten-year-old Mexican girl named Maria who was in a coma after being hit by a car. The doctors said there was nothing more they could do, and they sent her home, still unconscious. For nearly seven months she remained comatose. No one knew if she would ever recover.

Then, on July 27, 1976, a stray cat came through her open bedroom window. He was probably looking for food and a comfortable bed. Francesca, Maria's mother, wanted him to go. Then she noticed that the cat was carefully licking the girl's thumb, over and over. And as he licked, the girl's fingers began to twitch. *Wake up, Maria. Wake up*, her mother prayed. She named the cat Miguel and encouraged him to stay. For over a week, Miguel visited Maria, snuggling by her side and grooming her hand. On the eighth day, Maria awoke.

She recovered so rapidly that her parents decided to take her on a vacation to the United States. They told the housekeeper to put food and drink for Miguel in Maria's room and to leave the bedroom window open so he could come and go. But when they returned two weeks later, the cat had disappeared, never to return. Maybe he thought his friend had gone for good and so he too should depart. Or perhaps his work there was complete and he'd left to find someone else to help.

Not all feline therapists have performed feats as dramatic as awakening people from comas or encouraging Alzheimer's patients to speak. But their treatment has been impressive all the same. One such feline therapist cured a nearly disastrous case of stage fright.

APPLAUSE, APPLAUSE!

Ignacy Paderewski was terrified when he stepped onstage at the Saint James's Hall to make his London debut in 1890. How would he ever get through that first piece? He feared that his career would be over before it started. Tense, he sat down at the piano. Then, to his surprise, the theater's cat strolled out and jumped onto his lap. The audience laughed with delight. The pianist began to relax—and to play. Throughout the whole étude, the puss stayed in place, purring. Paderewski's debut was a grand success! He went on to become a world-famous musician. Later he gave credit where it was due—to the music-loving cat therapist who cured his stage fright.

Other musicians, painters, and writers can thank a slew of felines not only for being therapists and companions, but also for being inspirations. I'm one of them. My cats soothe and cheer me. They've also suggested ideas for poems, stories, and, of course, this book. Do they know? I doubt it. Do they care? Maybe. Writing makes me happy, and, as every cat knows, a happy companion is good company.

Chapter 11

🐈

Muse

CATARINA

The tortoiseshell cat sat contentedly on the author's shoulder. She didn't know that he was writing a dark tale about a man who kills both his cat and his wife, and she didn't care. It was true that her master was a moody fellow, sometimes prone to drinking and odd behavior. But Catarina adored him, and she knew he was equally fond of her. "Perhaps this new collection will make us rich," the writer may have told the cat.

Not so. The anthology of spooky stories was popular, but it didn't earn the author much money. In fact, he and his wife, Virginia, whom he deeply loved, were so poor that they couldn't afford a good quilt, let alone fuel. In the cold New York winter of 1846, the young woman lay on a straw bed wrapped only in her husband's coat. Catarina slept on her chest to keep them both warm. Though the feline tried her best, she could not save her mistress from tuberculosis. Virginia died the following year. A few years later, her husband also died. The money from his stories—lots of it—went to other people.

Today we are still reading "The Black Cat" and other chilling tales by Edgar Allan Poe. And although no one knows what became of Catarina, in a way she also achieved immortality as the author's four-legged muse.

PRACTICAL CATS

A muse is a being who offers artistic inspiration. A good muse can not only help artists come up with ideas, but also make them examine themselves and their behavior. To many people, cats seem to be content creatures who live in the here and now. They act like themselves at all times and never worry what people think of them. Others see cats as magical, with powers to heal or to avenge. Poe possibly saw felines as all of those things. In "The Black Cat," the creature avenges its own and its mistress's death, but the story is more about a man who becomes evil because of his addiction to alcohol and is haunted by his guilt. Poe hated his addiction, and so, in many ways, the story is really an attack on himself.

My own cats have made me ask questions about myself, too: Who am I? What makes me content? How can I worry less about the past or the future and really enjoy the present? What does it take to be a hero? Could I ever be one?

Many writers, as well as painters, composers, musicians, and other artists, have had feline muses. The British poet T. S. Eliot's pusses inspired *Old Possum's Book of Practical Cats*. That collection of poems in turn inspired Andrew Lloyd Webber's long-running musical *Cats*. French author Colette also owned many felines and wrote several works about them, including imaginary conversations between her gray Angora, Kiki-la-Doucette, and her French bulldog, Toby-Chien.

Mystery writer Raymond Chandler's Persian, Taki, always kept him company while he wrote. Sometimes she'd lean against the typewriter. Other times, in Chandler's words, she'd gaze out the window "as if to say, 'The stuff you're doing is a waste of time.'" Before revising, Chandler actually read his manuscripts aloud to Taki. He called her his "feline secretary."

Thanks to his cat Foss, Edward Lear, the well-known poet of limericks and other nonsense verse, wrote about the owl and the pussycat who "went to sea in a beautiful pea-green boat." Lear so loved Foss that, in 1881, when he decided to move from one villa to another in San Remo, Italy, he had the new house built to match his old one exactly so that the cat would feel at home. When Foss died at the age of seventeen, he was buried in the Italian garden, under a tombstone.

FOSS

Lear himself, deeply saddened, died just two months later at the age of seventy-six.

WALTZING FELINES, PAINTED PUSSYCATS

In the fields of music and painting, there are a host of compositions inspired by feline muses. Two of the best known are Domenico Scarlatti's "Cat Fugue" and Frédéric Chopin's "Cat's Waltz." Both were supposedly inspired by pusses who walked across the keyboards of a harpsichord and a piano, respectively. Leonardo da Vinci, renowned painter and inventor, often drew cats. He featured a feline with baby Jesus in his *Madonna and Child with a Cat*. Da Vinci said, "The smallest feline is a masterpiece." Many artists— and nonartists, as well—would agree with him. Cats are sleek and graceful, with shining fur and gleaming eyes. They're perfectly designed for all their tasks, and they're fun to watch, to draw, to sculpt, to film, and to imitate through sound, dance, or performance.

The best-known cat painter of his day was British artist Louis Wain. His first drawings were of a black-and-white kitten named Peter. These were published in the *Illustrated London News* in

Chapter II

1884. Later on, Wain cre-
ated humorous portraits
of cats in human dress,
as well as the first ani-
mated cat cartoon, *Pussy-
foot*, in 1916. As he grew
older, Wain began to act oddly and
was diagnosed with schizophrenia. He spent the
last fifteen years of his life in mental hospitals.
But he continued to paint cats, creating some of
his best—and strangest—work. Several of these
paintings feature muses that are no longer amusing. They have electric fur and flaming eyes or
kaleidoscopic patterns. As one critic said, they
seem to glow with a "magical fire."

To some people, felines have always been
magical. And therein lies another cat tale. . . .

Chapter 12

God, Goddess, Monarch, Magician

SINH

Mun-Ha, the head monk, sat serenely in the temple on Mount Lugh before the statue of Tsun-Kyan-Kse, the golden goddess with the sapphire blue eyes. The goddess helped souls enter Nirvana—heaven. Every day Mun-Ha meditated in front of her. His beard, braided with gold, showed that he himself had been favored by the gods. At the monk's side was Sinh, his faithful white cat with the yellow eyes and brown paws, nose, and tail.

That night Mun-Ha was meditating so deeply he did not hear the invaders approaching the temple. He did not see them enter. He felt no pain when they killed him. Sinh was grief-stricken by his master's death, but his duty was not only to Mun-Ha, but also to Tsun-Kyan-Kse. The cat put his paws on the monk's robes, then jumped onto the holy throne and faced the goddess. As he gazed at her statue, his fur became golden and his eyes turned a rich, shining blue. His paws, which had touched his master, were now pure white.

Inspired by Sinh, the other *kittahs* — monks — were able to drive the invaders away. For a week, the cat did not leave the throne. Then, on the seventh day after Mun-Ha's death, Sinh also died. With him he carried the spirit of his master and delivered it to the goddess so that Mun-Ha could pass into Nirvana.

In the meantime, the temple's other ninety-nine cats had, like Sinh, been transformed. While the monks argued over who should take Mun-Ha's place as leader, the felines entered the room and surrounded the youngest *kittah*. He became Mun-Ha's successor.

Since then, the *kit-tahs* have believed that upon their deaths, Bir-man cats will bear their souls to heaven. To this day, you can find these cats in Burmese temples. All of them have dark faces, ears, legs, and tails; golden fur; pure white paws; and bright blue eyes.

MUMMIES AND MAGICIANS

Throughout history, many cultures have believed that cats possess special powers. After all, cats have amazing hunting skills and better senses than we do. Their eyes are large, luminous, and alien. Felines seem to have the ability to survive heat, drought, and accidents. They can sometimes, though not always, fall from high places and land on their feet. In fact, they stand a better chance of surviving falls from seven to thirty-two stories than from two to six stories. That's because the greater height gives them more chance to twist in the air and land on their feet. To some people, these abilities have made cats seem unlucky or evil, agents of the Devil. As a result, many cats in medieval Europe were tortured and killed. But to other people, cats' abilities showed that they were blessed by heavenly beings and that they brought good fortune.

As mentioned in the introduction, the ancient Egyptians worshipped cats. When a pet feline died, the household members shaved their eyebrows and went into mourning. Anyone who killed a cat was put to death, except for a priest sacrificing the feline in honor of Bastet, goddess of joy and pleasure (also known as Bast). All cats were sacred to her. Bastet was represented either by the figure of a woman with a cat's head or of a cat itself. Her temple stood in the city of Bubastis, where thousands of cat mummies were buried. Some were household cats who had died natural deaths; others were sacrifices. All were buried with honor and respect.

It is a sad fact that years later people decided the mummies were worthless. When they were unearthed, many of the mummies were ground into fertilizer. Fortunately, some survived, and today they are found in museums and universities, where researchers study them to reveal when and how the cats died and how they were mummified.

In Siam, now called Thailand, Siamese cats were also considered holy. When a king died, officials placed a Siamese cat into his tomb but cut a hole in the wall so it could escape. The people believed that when the animal emerged, it carried with it the king's soul. The feline then attended the crowning of the next king. For the rest of its life, its job was to watch and protect the new monarch. When the cat died, it bore the former king's soul to heaven. As recently as 1926, a cat was an honored guest at a Thai king's coronation.

THE BECKONING CAT

An ancient Japanese legend tells of another type of magical feline, the Maneki Neko, or Beckoning Cat. There are several tales about this being. One tells of a lord who, centuries ago, was traveling with his men near a temple. The weather was growing stormy, and they had stopped under some trees, and when the lord saw a cat beckoning in the temple doorway, he decided to follow it inside. Just as he and his samurai entered, a bolt of lightning struck the very tree under which he'd been standing. "You must be the goddess of mercy!" exclaimed the lord. From then on, he was the patron of the temple, endowing it with riches.

Today, the Gotokuji Temple still exists. It is called the Temple of Cats. Owners go there to pray for their pets. No real cats live there, but there are many carvings and statues of the Maneki Neko waving its paw. These statues are, in fact, sold throughout Japan. They are said to bring wealth and happiness and to welcome in good friends.

HOLY CATS

Some heroic cats have been associated with famous religious figures. The prophet Muhammad was believed to have adored cats because one saved his life. A snake had crawled into his sleeve and would not leave. Muhammad's cat arrived and told the snake to come out and discuss its departure. When the reptile poked out its head, the cat grabbed it and carried it away.

That cat might have been Muezza, Muhammad's favorite, featured in another story about the prophet. Several times a day Muhammad went to pray. But at one call to prayer he dis-

covered that Muezza was asleep on his sleeve
(perhaps the same one that had been once occu-
pied by the snake). Rather than awaken the cat,
Muhammad cut off the sleeve and quietly slipped
away. When he returned, Muezza showed his
gratitude and respect by arching his spine and
raising his tail. Muhammad then stroked the cat's
back three times, giving him nine lives and the
ability to land on his feet. Because of the prophet's
fondness for cats, felines have long been viewed
by Muslim people as clean and good. A cat is one
of the few animals allowed to enter paradise.

Another tale says that Francis of Assisi, patron
saint of animals, was also rescued by felines.
Francis came from a wealthy Italian family. He
had girlfriends, riches, power—everything a young
man could want. But he gave up all of it to live
a life of poverty and charity. One day during
his prayers, the Devil decided to test him. He
sent mice to nibble his toes and robe. When Francis did not budge, God sent a cat who jumped
from the saint's sleeve to kill all the mice. But two
mice escaped through a hole in the wall. To this
day, cats wait at mouseholes for the rodents to
appear.

STARGAZY PIE

Mousehole (pronounced "Mouzel") happens to be the name of a village in Cornwall, England. It's a small place with a narrow harbor entrance, rather like a mouse's hole. Legend has it that the town owes much to a heroic cat called Mouzer. She lived in a cottage with an old fisherman named Tom Bawcock. Every day they ate delicious fish that Tom had caught. But one winter the weather turned cold and stormy. The sea swelled, and the waves tossed the boats in the harbor like shells. People said that the dreaded Storm-Cat was stirring the waters. The villagers feared the Storm-Cat and wouldn't go fishing. Food grew more and more scarce.

On the night before Christmas Eve, Tom said to the cat, "Mouzer, everyone is starving. I am the oldest fisherman here. It is my duty to catch fish. If I drown, so be it. I have had a good, long life."

Mouzer could not bear the thought of her master going out alone in the storm. Unseen, she padded behind him to his boat and leaped inside. By the time Tom saw her, it was too late. The pair had set out to sea. Rain and spray beat down on

the little craft. Wind and
waves hurled it into the air.
Tom and Mouzer were
frightened, but the feline
would not abandon
her master. She
climbed to the prow
and began to sing.
She sang and sang
until the Storm-Cat paused

to listen. He became so entranced by her song
that he forgot to stir the waters. The rain and
wind stopped. The sea grew calm. Tom cast his
nets and drew them up, full of fish.

Still Mouzer kept singing until the whole boat
was laden with fish and she and Tom were safe in
the harbor. There on the dock the worried villagers waited with lanterns. When they saw the
pair, they let out a great cheer. Then they all hap-
pily marched to their homes to bake fish pies.

From then on, December 23 in Mousehole
became known as Tom Bawcock's Eve. If you
ever visit, stop at the inn and have a bit of star-
gazy pie featuring fish heads and tails in honor of
brave Tom and his heroic cat, Mouzer.

Chapter 13

Actor

PUSS-IN-BOOTS

There once was a young man (Andre, we'll call him) whose father died and left him nothing but a cat. "There's not even enough meat on you to make me a stew," he said sadly, petting the feline with affection and concern.

"Now, now. We can both do better than stew," the cat replied. "Give me a pair of boots and a pouch, and I will show you how."

How the young man acquired the boots and pouch is another story, but acquire them he did. And with his finery, the cat set out on the road to make their fortune. He quickly caught a rabbit.

But instead of bringing it to Andre, he took it to the king. "A gift," he told the monarch, "from the Marquis of Carabas."

The king was amused. But over time, as Puss-in-Boots brought more and more gifts from his master, the monarch's amusement turned to curiosity. He had never heard of this Marquis of Carabas (and neither had anyone else, though no one admitted it). At last, he told Puss that he and the princess were determined to meet the young lord the very next day.

"I'm doomed," said Andre, when the cat told him the news.

"Not at all," said Puss. "I am from a long line of theater cats. I will teach you to act the part of a lord, and, if you follow all that I say, your fortune will be made."

Andre agreed. Puss was a good teacher and he was a quick study. He soon learned how to speak and move the way a real marquis would.

At dawn, Puss and Andre set out for the palace. They hid in the bushes until they saw the royal carriage pull away with the king and the princess inside. Then Puss commanded Andre to take off his clothes and jump in the river.

Puss flung his rags behind a boulder and flagged down the carriage. "Sire, sire! Thieves have attacked my master and stolen his clothes."

"Oh, my!" said the king. He had his footmen rush back to his palace and return with a fine velvet suit, which fit Andre perfectly. When the young man appeared in his new clothes, the princess took one look and insisted that he ride with them in the carriage.

The cat did not join them. He had more work to do. Dashing ahead, he convinced peasants plowing fields and gathering fruit to tell the king that the fields and orchards belonged to the Marquis of Carabas.

Then Puss came to a big castle. It was owned by an ogre—and not a nice one. "I have heard so much about you" said Puss. "But my mother, rest her soul, taught me that not everything one hears is true. Surely you can't *really* change into a lion, now can you?"

"Oh, yeah?" said the ogre. Presto, he became a lion.

"Oh, my!" gasped Puss. "That's astounding! But surely you can't turn into something as tiny as a . . . let's say . . . a mouse."

"Oh, yeah?" repeated the ogre. His vocabulary was not very large. Neither was his brain. As soon as he turned into a mouse, Puss caught and ate him. When the king's carriage appeared at the gates, the cat flung them wide open and said, "Welcome to the home of the Marquis of Carabas."

If Andre was shocked, he didn't show it. And in a very short time, he was a marquis for real, one married to the lovely princess.

"I told you we could do better than stew," said Puss, licking caviar from his paws. "It's all a matter of"—he struck a pose. Andre imitated it.

"Acting!" they both exclaimed. Sweeping off their hats, they made deep bows.

THEATER CATS

The brilliant actor Puss-in-Boots is, of course, a fairy-tale hero. Although there are far fewer theater cats now than there used to be, cats have long lived in playhouses. Theater folk are known to have many superstitions, some about felines. We've all heard of black cats bringing bad luck. Among actors, opera singers, stagehands, and other theater people, the opposite is true — a black cat is supposed to bring success. Cats of other colors are lucky, too. Years ago, some actors believed that if a theater cat rubbed against them, they'd become famous in no time. I suspect that today there are performers who still believe this superstition.

Cats accidentally appearing *during* a play have sometimes brought good fortune as well. In his classic book about cats, *A Tiger in the House*, Carl Van Vechten tells this story: In 1906, playwright Channing Pollock was attending the opening of his newest work, *The Little Gray Lady*. No one was laughing at the jokes. The play was going to be a flop. Then, Act II began. The scene was a backyard with a fence, an alley, and a garbage can. Suddenly, the theater cat, unrehearsed, jumped over the fence and into the can. When he found it empty, he jumped out again and walked down the alley off-stage. The audience burst into laughter and applauded. From then on, they enjoyed the play. So, for all the following performances, the stage-hands laid a trail of hamburger along the route and got the cat to repeat his actions night after night. That puss turned *The Little Gray Lady* into a hit.

London's longest serving theater cat was Beerbohm of the Globe Theatre (now called the Gielgud Theatre). An excellent mouser, Beerbohm occasionally wandered onstage during a play, which pleased the audience, though not the actors. He died at the age of twenty in 1995.

From 1984 to 2003, the Church Street Theater in Washington, D.C., had a resident cat called Gus, named for Gus the Theatre Cat in T. S. Eliot's poem. The gray tabby was known to appear onstage whenever he felt like it—usually in scenes that did not require a cat. He also tracked paw prints through newly painted sets and caused other trouble. But everyone loved him just the same. Gus helped the acting students by appearing onstage during their classes. Peter Frisch, their teacher, would tell the students to work the cat into the scene. In that way, Gus taught them how to improvise.

MOVIE STARS

Gus, Beerbohm, and other theater cats were not really actors. But some talented cats are. We've all seen the white Persians that advertise Fancy Feast cat food or play Snowball in the Stuart Little films (there were six cats for that one role) and finicky Morris, the orange tabby who sells 9 Lives cat food on TV. These cats have all been trained to perform. Some, like Morris, came from animal shelters and were adopted by trainers who knew that these felines had the right qualities to be actors. The first Morris's real name was Lucky. His owner claimed the cat was just twenty minutes away from being put to death in a shelter when he was rescued. Since his death from natural causes in 1975, there have been several other Morrises. In 1988 and 1992 the cat ran for president of the United States on the Finicky Party ticket. His campaign issue was good nutrition for felines. The current Morris appears in stores all over the country to sell his brand of cat food, but also to donate it to shelters. Morris and his trainers have never forgotten his humble beginnings.

PRINCESS KITTY

Princess Kitty was a stray brown-and-white kitten who adopted Karen Payne. The kitten had a nasty personality and often bit people. Karen decided that training was the answer. Princess Kitty learned nearly one hundred tricks, including playing a toy piano and dunking a little basketball. Her personality changed. From 1986 to 2003, she performed for children at schools and hospitals. She wasn't bothered by noise or crowds, and she loved kids. Though Princess Kitty is gone, Karen still writes a cat training column. She feels that her remarkable feline showed that cats can do and be more than people ever thought was possible.

And she's right. Dogs may be easier to train —

they like to please their human pack leader and receive praise and treats—but cats, too, can be taught tricks and skills. Trainers pick outgoing cats and see what they do naturally. Then they reinforce and shape that behavior using clickers, praise, and treats. Each time the cat does the right activity, the trainer clicks the clicker, then quickly gives the feline a treat. Eventually, the cat learns to do the trick without the treat. Zoo-keepers use clicker training with big cats so that the animals will allow veterinarians to examine and care for them. For example, a clicker-trained tiger can be taught to turn around and offer its tail through an opening in a cage. Then the vet can easily give it an injection. House cats can be clicker trained to do a variety of activities, even agility—running an obstacle course with jumps, tunnels, ramps, and other equipment.

Performing cats can provide entertainment and therapy. They make good role models, inspiring people to solve problems with their own felines through training rather than punishment or giving the pet away. Unlike Puss-in-Boots, a trained cat probably won't get you fame and for-tune—but then again, it just might!

Chapter 14

Jack-of-All-Trades

MAGGIE

Today was the day. The kids were old enough. Toby was nine, and Belinda was seven. They'd promised to share the responsibility of caring for a dog, and their parents believed them. There was just one problem—Felix, their cat. For two years, he'd been the only four-legged mammal in the Mooneys' house. But soon he'd have to share that honor with a pesky canine!

The Mooneys were thoughtful people. They'd done a lot of research, and they had a plan. Together they'd go to the Pasadena Humane Society to pick out a pup. But not just any pup. No matter how cute the canine was, they would only adopt it if Maggie, the Humane Society's house cat, approved. She would tell them whether or not Felix would approve, too.

At the animal shelter, the Mooneys looked at several dogs. "This one!" said Toby. "Too big," said his dad. "How about her?" Mrs. Mooney exclaimed. "Too small!" sniffed Toby.

Then Belinda spotted a medium-size brown pup with big, shiny eyes. "Ooh, look!" She pointed. "Awww," her family chorused.

"Let's see what Maggie has to say," said the friendly counselor who worked there. She brought the pup and the Mooneys into another room. On the table sat a tabby cat. "Well, Maggie," said the counselor, "what do you think?"

The Mooneys held their breath. The cat stared at the dog and gave a deep meow. The pup's ears stood up. He began to wag his tail.

"He likes her!" Belinda cried.

"Yes, and Maggie knows it. This dog will work out fine in your home," said the counselor.

"Hooray!" Belinda cheered. So did her family. They brought the pup home and named him Rags. Felix sulked under the bed for two days. Then he came out and took over Rags's new bed. Rags didn't mind at all. From that day on, the pair got along just fine. Maggie the Dog Tester had been right—again!

The Mooneys, Felix, and Rags are all made-up characters. But Maggie was real. Found in a Dumpster when she was only a month old, she became a permanent resident at the Pasadena Humane Society in California, wandering through the education and volunteer offices whenever she liked. In 1996, she began to earn her keep, becoming the world's first recorded dog-testing feline. From then until her death in 2001, she told prospective adopters whether or not a dog was likely to be compatible with their cats. If a canine acted aggressive toward her, the adopters were advised to look around the shelter for another dog. Maggie was never in any danger—she was free to walk away, while each dog was on a leash.

Calm, curious, and friendly, Maggie was the perfect puss for her unusual job. She tested four or five dogs daily and was responsible for thousands of successful adoptions. To date, the Pasadena Humane Society has not yet found a replacement for her. She was a unique cat with a unique career. But everyone hopes that someday soon another cat will appear and follow in her heroic footsteps.

PEPURR AND THE GRAND
COULEE DAM CAT

Maggie insured that many cats would not feel unhappy about their new canine companions. PePurr has insured that a number of cats are still *alive*. This black-and-white feline, who lives at the Cat Hospital in Northampton, Massachusetts, has a highly important job—he is the resident feline blood donor. Approximately once every six weeks, he supplies fresh blood—two and a half ounces at a time — for cats who need it because of accidents, disease, or surgery. The procedure is painless — PePurr is always sedated, and his body quickly replaces the donated blood.

Veterinarian Maureen Ricksgers feels that PePurr also donates part of his personality to cats in need. In 2003, PePurr's blood saved the life of a dying cat. As the patient improved, his personality changed. He became tough and playful, just like PePurr! At the hospital, PePurr gets good food and lots of attention. Grateful pet owners have also given him many gifts. Does he enjoy his life and his job? If he could speak, he'd probably answer, "What's not to like?"

Because of their size, intelligence, and personalities, cats have been able to fill a wide variety of unusual roles. Some, like Maggie and PePurr, have long-term jobs. Other cats perform just one courageous task and then their work is done. One such cat showed up out of the blue to help build the Grand Coulee Dam.

By 1942, engineers had been constructing the dam across Washington State's Columbia River for nine years. It was going to be 550 feet high, if they ever finished it. But they were stuck with a problem. They couldn't figure out a way to run a cable through five hundred feet of narrow, crooked, partially blocked drainage pipe. Then one engineer noticed a small, friendly white female cat nosing around. She let him tie some string to her tail. Attached to the string was the cable. When the engineer placed her in the pipe, she curiously moved forward. Then he shot a gentle blast of air at her rear end to make her keep going, pulling the cable with her. When she came out the other side, the crew cheered.

Hopefully, they gave her some treats and a good home, because without that little puss, the world's largest concrete structure might never have been completed.

POLITICAL PUSSYCATS

Maggie, PePurr, and the Grand Coulee cat are examples of behind-the-scenes heroes. Socks, Humphrey, and Slippers were all public figures. Socks and Slippers shared the White House with, respectively, Bill Clinton and Teddy Roosevelt. Humphrey lived at 10 Downing Street through the terms of several British prime ministers. Popular and well-photographed, these felines raised interest and often funds for cats worldwide. They provided amusing stories for the press, made national and international guests feel comfortable (and occasionally uncomfortable, too), and helped make their residences more homey. There have been many other presidential cats. Abraham Lincoln, Calvin Coolidge, John F. Kennedy, and George W. Bush have had pet felines. Rutherford B. Hayes owned the first Siamese cat in the United States.

Prime Minister Winston Churchill of Great Britain had several felines, including a large black fellow named Nelson. One day during World War II, Churchill came down with the flu. He was in bed with Nelson curled up on his feet. A cabinet minister came to visit him. When the minister seemed a bit put off by the cat, Churchill retorted, "This cat does more for the war effort than you do. He acts as a hot water bottle and saves fuel and power."

Though these cats have lived with politicians, no one would call them government leaders. But in Guffey, Colorado, cats do rule—for real. Since the mid-1980s, four of them have served as the town's mayor. Several years ago, the residents were discussing how to get more attention for their town. One resident, Donna Arnink, suggested that they appoint a cat as mayor. The deputy sheriff, Betty Royse, was heard to say they might as well, for all the good it would do them. The citizens decided that was a fine idea, so they elected a calico named Paisley, owned by Judy Robbins. The appointment gave the town so much publicity that the county took notice and paved some of the roads and installed private phone lines. The residents built a community center. Paisley was off to a fine start.

Next came a Persian/Siamese mix called Smudge LaPlume. She helped get some roads repaired. When Smudge was killed by a coyote,

Wiffy LaGone, another calico, took over. The population of the town rose to twenty-six folks. In 1993, when the "mayor's office" (the general store) was bought by a new owner, the "Democats" lost out to a self-appointed "Repupkin": Shanda, the new owner's golden retriever. But on Halloween in 1998, the citizens felt there should be a real election. This time, Monster, a friendly black cat, won fair and square, beating out two dogs and a cockatiel. Who knows what he will accomplish in office, but as far as the residents of Guffey are concerned, he's already done a fine job of eating, sleeping, purring, and keeping the town in the news. And in case anything should happen to him, there's Monster 2, another black cat, in training to take over the demanding job!

Chapter 15

Survivor

PRECIOUS

Precious sat in her favorite window, staring at the twin towers across the way. The white Persian cat had never been out of doors, but that didn't bother her. Nor was she troubled by the fact that her people were out of town. The pet sitter would arrive soon to take excellent care of her. In fact, Precious thought she had nothing to worry about on that lovely, sunny morning, September 11, 2001.

Then came the deafening noise and the shaking, the flying glass and metal, the dust and smoke. In too short and too terrible a time, the

World Trade Center lay in ruins. Many lives were lost. Precious's building was severely damaged, and the cat was gone.

Or so her owners D.J. and Steve Kerr thought. Seventeen dreadful days passed. Hope grew more and more slim for finding any survivors of the disaster. But on the eighteenth day, a worker was assembling lights on the roof of the Kerrs' building to aid the recovery effort below. He thought he heard a meowing somewhere and he asked the rescue team to help. The team sent for a Search and Rescue (SAR) dog. With the canine's help, they found the thin, scared cat. Precious had sores in her mouth from drinking rainwater out of contaminated puddles, her eyes were injured, and her paws were burned from the hot tarmac. But to the joy of the Kerrs, the veterinarian said she would recover. The Westchester Cat Show named Precious "Cat of the Year." And everyone called her a miracle.

TOUGH COOKIES

There are countless stories of cats who, through strength, determination, and resourcefulness, manage to beat the odds. The felines that lived through Hurricane Katrina are recent examples. One cat that was both a survivor and a lifesaver was Miss Kitty.

On August 29, 2005, Bill Harris was awakened by her pitiful meowing atop the china cabinet. He discovered that an enormous storm surge had hit his condominium in Slidell, Louisiana. There was six feet of water in the room and his bed was being swept toward the broken bay window.

Bill plunged into the water. He could not get out the front door. It was blocked by a thirty-foot fishing boat that had landed on his porch. He was certain he was about to drown. Then he saw Miss Kitty leap across the room onto a table. He managed to reach it and was amazed to find an upright chair. Holding the cat in his arms, he scrambled onto the chair and stood there for three days, calling over and over for help.

When the rescuers finally arrived, they refused to reenter the condo to get the cat. Distraught, Bill was taken to a shelter. Several days passed. Two brave volunteers, Donna Wackerbauer of Noah's Wish, an animal rescue group, and Slidell

animal officer Horace Trouiller, set out to find
Miss Kitty. They did—and cat and owner had a
joyous reunion. Sadly, it was short-lived. Because
of his poor health, Bill had to move to a nursing
home that did not allow animals. On November
23 he died.

Miss Kitty, however, is doing fine. She has a
new home up north in Canada with her rescuer,
Donna Wackenbauer, and nine new canine and
feline companions, including three other Katrina
survivors: Boudoin, a dog found in a pile of debris;
Cullion, a kitten with birth defects; and Funk, a
cat named after the license plate of the truck
where he was found hiding between the tailgate
and the bumper.

CAN YOU DIG IT?

Like Funk, other cats have been found alive after
spending days or even weeks locked in store-
rooms, drawers, shipping containers, or even vend-
ing machines. Others survive after being trapped
behind walls or buried in the ground. In 1992 in
Minnesota, a yellow tabby named Marty was
frightened by the men working on the patio at his

family's apartment building. He decided to hide in a hole until they left. He didn't expect the workmen, not knowing he was there, to cover his secret place with a ten-inch slab of wet concrete.

Marty's owners, the Dunbars, were puzzled and upset by their cat's disappearance. Their eight-year-old son, Frankie, cried for days. What would he do without his good feline friend? Then, eleven days later, Frankie and his parents heard a sound at the patio door and went to look outside. There, covered with dirt, was Marty. His paws were muddy and he had no more claws. It took a while to figure out what had happened— Marty had stubbornly scratched and dug his way out of the hole. He had probably gotten enough air by following the routes mice used underground. Whether he'd also eaten any of those mice, no one knows.

Tigger was another cat that dug his way to freedom. He lived in Devon, England, with Nurse Caridwin Jones, three other cats, and a parakeet. One night in February 2002, the tabby did not return home. Caridwin worried that he'd been stolen or, worse, that he'd been buried in a landslide when a wall had collapsed near the home of her neighbors, Derek Hope and Wendy Howard. She put up posters and sent out a message over the radio asking for help in his return. But no one responded and there was no sign of Tigger. Several difficult weeks passed, and the nurse began to fear she'd never see him again.

One midnight, after Tigger had been gone a month, Caridwin's neighbors Derek and Wendy heard a scraping at their half-open window. The couple rose to see what was happening. To their amazement, a ragged, skinny cat was attempting to enter their room. Wendy rushed to bring the poor feline inside. She recognized Tigger even in his skeletal condition.

Derek suggested that, like Marty, the cat had found an air pocket and had also found water droplets to lick. But he had not found food. Oddly enough, his thinness may have helped save his life. The skinnier he got, the more he could squeeze through narrow spaces in the rubble. How many lives did he use up by being buried for a month? At least four, Caridwin said.

How do cats survive such terrible conditions? They live off stored fat, as do all mammals. They can find the smallest amounts of water, and their little barbed tongues allow them to drink the droplets. They have determination and intelligence. They don't fear tight, dark places, and they don't give up easily.

We think of these survivors as heroes — especially the ones that struggled to live through national disasters. They cast a small but cheerful light in a dark time.

HOPE

That's why Precious made the news, as did another 9/11 feline survivor. Thin and ill, she was found in the basement beneath what had been a restaurant in the World Trade Center area of downtown New York City. She was sleeping in a

carton of napkins, and she was not alone. With her were three kittens.

At the animal shelter, the veterinarians said that all of them would recover and go to good homes—and so they did. The kittens were named

Freedom, Amber, and Flag. The mother was called Hope, a fitting name for a cat who helped affirm that, despite all the sorrow, the world is still a good place.

How to Be a
Hero to Your Cat

Sir Isaac Newton, who suggested the theory of gravity, among other things, is considered to be a hero by many people. He was also a hero to his cat. The feline demanded constantly to be let out and to come in, so the great scientist invented the first cat flap door.

Our cats give us affection, amusement, and companionship. In return they deserve to be treated well. How can we provide them with the best care? By feeding them a proper diet. By stroking them and giving them good attention. By taking them to the veterinarian for regular checkups. By supplying them with toys, treats, and other things to prevent boredom. By keeping them safe so that they don't get hit by a car, attacked by predators, or exposed to disease. And by spaying or neutering them.

Every day in the United States alone, thousands of kittens are born. Many are unwanted. Homeless cats roam countless cities, towns, and rural areas. Animal shelters are full of cats no one will adopt. Each year millions of them will be killed. To help solve this problem, unless you are a qualified breeder, you can make sure your cat will not father or mother kittens. Even if you have homes for them, there are already too many kittens who need good places to live. Many veterinarians have low-cost spay/neuter programs. So do organizations such as Friends of Animals. Shelters generally offer spaying and neutering for free or for a small fee when you adopt a pet.

So, be a hero to your cat. Give it the best possible life, and who knows? Puss may someday be a hero to you.

Bibliography

For research, I read a great many articles and books about cats. Here are some of them.

BOOKS:

Altman, Roberta. *The Quintessential Cat*. New York: Macmillan, 1994.

Anderson, Janice. *The Cat-a-logue*. Enfield, UK: Guinness Books, 1989.

Barber, Antonia, and Nicola Bayley (illust.). *The Mousehole Cat*. New York: Macmillan Publishing Co., 1990.

Beadle, Muriel. *The Cat: History, Biology, and Behavior*. New York: Simon & Schuster, 1977.

Bonners, Susan. *Why Does the Cat Do That?* New York: Henry Holt & Co., 1998.

Capuzzo, Michael, and Teresa Banik Capuzzo. *Cat Caught My Heart: Stories of Wisdom, Hope, and Purrfect Love*. New York: Bantam Books, 1998.

Caras, Roger A. *A Cat Is Watching*. New York: Simon & Schuster, 1989.

Comfort, David. *The First Pet History of the World*. New York: Simon & Schuster, 1994.

Dohanyos, Franklin, ed. *The Cats of Our Lives: Funny and Heartwarming Reminiscences of Feline Companions*. Secaucus, NJ: Birch Lane Press, 1999.

Fogle, Dr. Bruce. *The Cat's Mind: Understanding Your Cat's Behavior*. New York: Howell Book House, 1992.

Gaddis, Vincent and Margaret. *The Strange World of Animals and Pets*. New York: Cowles Book Co., 1979.

Greene, David. *Your Incredible Cat: Understanding the Secret Powers of Your Pet*. Garden City, NY: Doubleday, 1986.

Hausman, Gerald and Loretta, *The Mythology of Cats: Feline Legend and Love Through the Ages*. New York: St. Martin's Press, 1998.

Holmgren, Virginia C. *Cats in Fact and Folklore*. New York: Howell Book House, 1996.

Jay, Roni. *The Kingdom of the Cat*. Buffalo, NY: Firefly Books, 2000.

Laland, Stephanie. *Animal Angels: Amazing Acts of Love and Compassion*. Berkeley, CA: Conari Press, 1998.

Lewis, Margaret. *Wild Discovery Guide to Your Cat: Understanding and Caring for the Tiger Within*. London: Discovery Communications, 1999.

Loxton, Howard. *99 Lives: Cats in History, Legend and Literature*. San Francisco: Chronicle Books, 1998.

Masson, Jeffrey Moussaieff. *The Nine Emotional Lives of Cats: A Journey into the Feline Heart*. New York: Ballantine Books, 2002.

Méry, Fernand. *The Life, History and Magic of the Cat*. New York: Madison Square Press, 1966.

Nash, Bruce, and Allan Zullo. *Amazing but True Cat Tales*. Kansas City, MO: Andrews and McMeel, 1993.

Sayer, Angela. *The Encyclopedia of the Cat*. New York: Crescent Books, 1979.

Sheldrake, Rupert. *Dogs That Know When Their Owners Are Coming Home: And Other Unexplained Powers of Animals*. New York: Three Rivers Press, 1999.

Shojai, Amy. *The Incomparable Cat*. Leicester, UK: Magna Books, 1995.

Steiger, Brad. *Cats Incredible!: True Stories of Fantastic Feline Feats*. New York: Penguin Books, 1994.

Steiger, Brad, and Sherry Hansen Steiger. *Cat Miracles: Inspiring True Tales of Remarkable Felines*. Avon, MA: Adams Media Corp., 2003.

Suares, Jean-Claude. *The Indispensable Cat*. New York: Stewart, Tabori & Chang, 1983.

Swanson, Eric. *Hero Cats: True Stories of Daring Feline Deeds*. Kansas City, MO: Andrews McMeel Publishing, 1998.

Tabor, Roger. *Roger Tabor's Cat Behavior: A Complete Guide to Understanding How Your Cat Works*. Pleasantville, NY: Reader's Digest, 1998.

Van Vechten, Carl. *The Tiger in the House*. New York: Bonanza Books, 1920.

Von Kreisler, Kristin. *The Compassion of Animals: True Stories of Animal Courage and Kindness*. Rocklin, CA: Prima Publishing, 1997.

WEB SITES AND ONLINE ARTICLES:

www.pbs.org/wnet/nature/excats (PBS site on cats)

http://rulingcatsanddogs.com/facts-cat-main.htm (general site)

www.pawsonline.info/index.htm (general site)

www.moggies.co.uk/index.html (general site; Towser is featured at www.moggies.co.uk/misc/glenturret.html; Scarlett is featured at www.moggies.co.uk/html/scarlett.html)

www.catnews.com (general site)

http://www.shopcat.com (working cats; Matilda is featured at www.shopcat.com/algonquin/matilda.htm)

www.mountwashington.org/photos/cats/index.html (Nin)

www.cwgcuser.org.uk/personal/moggies/simon/simon.htm (Simon)

Bibliography

www.battleshipbismarck.hypermart.net/cat_oscar.htm (Oscar)

www.sonic.net/~pauline/psych.html (psi-trailing)

http://www.purr-n-fur.org.uk/famous/index.htm (Faith is featured at www.purr-n-fur.org.uk/famous/faith.html)

www.laceyville.com/Aggie/Book.htm (Aggie)

www.nationalgeographic.com/ngkids/9702/bear/ (Griz and Cat)

www.catworld.co.uk/articlecatworld.asp?artid=278&cat=General+Features&pre=0 (cats in music and song)

www.lilitu.com/catland/gallery.shtml and www.outsiderart.co.uk/wain.htm (Louis Wain's work)

http://pio.tripod.com/magicpaw/catmyths.html (Cats and World Mythology)

www.yabz.com/km/royal.html (King of Siam and cat)

www.princesskitty.com (Princess Kitty)

www.cnn.com/US/9703/26/fringe/cat (Maggie)

www.noho.com/pepurr (PePurr)

Index